Cuttlefish, Clones and Cluster Bombs

Cuttlefish, Clones and Cluster Bombs

Preaching, Politics and Ecology

Michael S. Northcott

DARTON·LONGMAN+TODD

First published in 2010 by
Darton, Longman and Todd Ltd
1 Spencer Court
140 – 142 Wandsworth High Street
London SW18 4JJ

ISBN 978-0-232-52798-8

A catalogue record for this book is available from the British Library.

Phototypeset by Kerrypress Ltd, Luton, Bedfordshire.
Printed and bound in Great Britain by Thomson Litho, East Kilbride, Scotland

Contents

Introduction   1

Advent
1. States of Alert   14
2. Creating Hunger and Growing Food   19

Christmas
3. Simeon and the Clone   28

Epiphany
4. The Return of the King   34

Lent
5. Happiness and Faithfulness   40
6. Foot-and-mouth and the Market   48

Passiontide
7. The Cross and the Cluster Bomb   56

Easter
8. Crosses, Crusaders and Peacemakers   62
9. Resurrection Fishing   70
10. The Hallowing of Time   76

Ascension
11. The Best Things in Life are Free   86
12. Absence and Ambiguity   91

Pentecost

13.	Pentecostal Politics	100
14.	The Global Corporation and the Body Politic	105

Trinity

15.	The Mandate of Heaven and the Divine Trinity	112

Creation Time

16.	The Earth Remains Forever	120
17.	The Climate of Communion	124
18.	Fishers, Salmon and Sustainable Food	132

St Francistide

19.	The Original Environmentalist?	141

Ordinary Time

20.	Hospitality and the Great Game	150
21.	Bowling Alone	158
22.	The Politics of Gentleness	165
23.	Poverty, Empire and History	171
24.	Calvin, Benedict and the Credit Crunch	178
25.	Trust and Obey	185
26.	Global Scattering and Christian Communion	190
27.	Health, Safety and Salvation	199
28.	Inequality and the Good Society	205
29.	Arms and Ploughshares	210
30.	The Divine Bias toward Children	218
31.	The Return of the Wolf	224
32.	Healing Hospitality	230

Introduction

The word was made flesh and dwelt among us.

John 1:14

The words inscribed on a stone lintel above the side door on a well-hidden church hall, where many of the sermons that follow were preached, say 'all are welcome here'. They indicate that, provided you can find the door at the end of a long path through a small side gate off of Leith Links in Scotland, you will find a welcome at the Episcopal Church of St James, whether atheist, Buddhist or Christian. These words are a political statement. The church is not a private club or a gathering of friends. It meets in public, at a time that is publicised on a notice board and on the worldwide web, and you do not have to be a member to find a welcome there. That is hopefully true of this book of sermons as well. Preached at particular times and places, they represent the traditional form of communication that Christians have practiced since the first days of the church in Jerusalem, and which they inherited – like so much else in the Christian way – from the Jews. They are offered here, in the form of a book, in the belief that they may offer some insight on the way to those who were not present on the occasions when they were preached.

That they are available in written form is testament paradoxically to their virtual existence on the worldwide web. In my first years at St James I was not accustomed to writing my sermons out in full, preferring short headings from which I would speak 'off the cuff' in a way that suited the style of worship there. But the church under the leadership of the second Rector with whom I worked, Steve Butler, developed a website. And on the site many of our sermons, or 'reflections' as they were often called, were posted so that members of the congregation could read them again, and so that those not present could catch up on the sermons they had missed. Hence even when I did not write a sermon out word for word beforehand, I increasingly found I wrote them out afterwards.

Karl Barth famously said that the preacher should always hold together two texts when she preaches – the Word of God, and the words of the daily newspaper. For in that juxtaposition she will find a place from which to declare the truth of God to a world where truth is a rare commodity. Barth's words help prevent too much attention to the daily news, especially for preachers who may from day to day read more of the newspaper than of any other text, though in what follows the reader will find perhaps more attention to the daily news than is customary. Barth's advice reflects the seriousness with which he took his first vocation as a preacher of the divine Word. The first duty of the preacher is to hear and study the Word of God as revealed truth and not just the words of human beings. The Word, as Barth so often emphasised, has a prophetic power that challenges the idols and shibboleths of every human era. It enters into every setting, every life, as an *un*common word, which, like Christ who is the divine Word, enters the world from another realm.

Barth's *Church Dogmatics* is a work of great imaginative power. And its driving metaphor is a given story, the story of the Prodigal Son, who goes from his father's house to a far country where he is not welcome, and who after enduring the trials of sin and the torments of wickedness, returns home to a father's festive welcome. In Barth's theology Christ the divine Word is the Prodigal Son who journeys from home to a far country mired in sin, and yet remains sinless and so redeems a prodigal world. In Barth's telling the world in the divine Word acquires a new story. Providence does this by making strange – the Incarnate Word is 'not of the world'. And hence the duty of the preacher, week by week, is to embrace the holy strangeness of the grace-filled words of Scripture in the midst of the familiarity of a prodigal world. This juxtaposition requires attention to the words of Scripture, with the aid of scriptural commentary and spiritual theology. And it requires attention to the *world*.

Barth's words indicate to the preacher the duty she has to make connections – figural and material – between the Word of God and the contemporary world. And this duty, when taken seriously, guards the preacher against a temptation which is all too common in certain circles and this is to attend exclusively to the task of expounding the meaning of the words of Scripture without attending to the situation of the congregation. In *Between Two Worlds* John Stott underlines the duty of the preacher to build a bridge within the sermon between the world of the Bible and the contemporary world. It is wrong, Stott suggests, to expect that those who are listening will themselves build such a bridge when the preacher has sought to stay only in one world, the world of Scripture.[1] The preacher has to work between two horizons – the Word and the world. But when facing the world the preacher, unlike the journalist, has the responsibility not only of immanent critique but of immanent construction. The preacher knows that another world has already been revealed, and that there *is* an alternative. And the preacher's task is not to suggest that one day in glory this world will be revealed. No. It is to find a golden thread between the Word and the lives of the people of God, and so to identify the forms in which the 'new creation' is already breaking in to the present world. Preaching in this sense is eschatological if not utopian. The preacher stands before the people of God not to condemn or to judge but to encourage them in thought and practice that the presence of God is already at work in the Church, in their lives, and in the world, redeeming, restoring, making whole.

Barth's advice to the preacher reminds those of us who live in societies where only a small minority of people gather on Sunday to worship God that preaching remains a form of *public* utterance, addressed to Christian citizens and to the world beyond the door of the church; that preaching remains a *political* act. Christians in the West increasingly encounter a political and social order that is neglectful of its Christian history and roots. Democracy, economics, education, the family, marriage, material

---

1   John R. W. Stott, *Between Two Worlds: The Art of Preaching in the Twentieth Century* (Grand Rapids, MI: Eerdmans, 1982).

progress, the nation state, private property, the public square, therapeutic care, limited war – all have their origins in the Christian West in the worshipful gathering of Christians Sunday by Sunday to hear and receive God's holy Word, to praise their maker and redeemer, to exchange the peace, and to share the Eucharist. From such gatherings emerged institutions and practices such as almsgiving, beekeeping, botany, canon law, convocations of clergy and laity, craft guilds, democratic debate, double-entry bookkeeping, gothic architecture, herbalism, hospitals, magistrates, marriage, mechanical inventions, public meetings, schools, sheep farming, universities, and war restrained by law. Liberal societies train their citizens that the practices and values of the modern State emanate from secular reason and are sustained by secular institutions such as the rule of law, market economics, multi-party democracy, public education, and a free press. But as the roots of the secular in the sacred are denied or forgotten, so the institutions and practices birthed by the Christian way are increasingly at risk of withering on the vine, cut off from the sustaining virtues of compassion and peaceableness, equity and justice, which Christians Sunday by Sunday rehearse and reclaim in the uncommon words of Scripture.

When I am not a preacher I work in the School of Divinity in the University of Edinburgh as a theologian. And some of my fellow theologians have sought to invent a new form of theology to address the growing gap between the secular and the theological which they call 'public theology'. But in medieval Scotland, or Puritan New England, *preaching* was public theology, and theologians were also preachers. The idea of a 'public theology' indicates that there is some form of theology that is not public; that theological speech can take the form of a private discourse, reserved for scholarly conferences and classrooms, journals and monographs, but not available as a resource for, or addressed to, the world. And theologians in the twentieth century took up their craft in this form of private speech in the university where it did much damage to the preaching of the Word. For those who would be preachers mostly study theology – at universities, in theological colleges or on training courses staffed by holders of university doctorates. And under the tutelage of modern theologians the Word is literally made strange to the aspirant preacher. The strangeness is not the contrast between the new world revealed in Scripture and the modern world. Instead it is the contrast between a naïve non-expert reading of Scripture and the reading of Scripture as subjected to the dominating power of scientific reason.

As Andrew Louth argues in *Discerning the Mystery*, the attempt to subject the study of Scripture to methods analogous to the experimental methods of the natural sciences produces considerable scepticism about the links between scriptural narratives and historical events.[2] It leads to an emphasis on the putatively 'primitive' worldview of scriptural texts, which is compared unfavourably with modern rationalist and science-informed worldviews. These methods also generate a focus on individual scriptural 'pericopes' in an attempt to envisage an original pre-canonical cultural setting or *sitz im leben* in which such pericopes are said to have originally been composed, first in oral and only later in written form. This produces a form of commentary in the twentieth century in which scholars treat particular books as edited snippets of oral and folk traditions which they claim to make more meaningful through their efforts to imagine and reconstruct the original *sitz im leben*. Such exegesis is a private scholarly enterprise conducted by professional theologians. And it resulted in the theft of Scripture from the churches because it trained generations of post-war preachers to treat of the Bible as a patchwork of sayings and stories with no divinely authored or ecclesial logic. These developments led to the silencing of the Bible in liberal churches. And they underscored pietistic and anti-intellectual tendencies in evangelical and con-

---

2 Andrew Louth, *Discerning the Mystery: An Essay on the Nature of Theology* (Oxford: Oxford University Press, 1983).

servative churches. The result is what Hans Frei called the 'eclipse of biblical narrative', or what Richard Neuhaus called the 'naked public square'.[3]

In contemporary biblical studies things look rather different. What is often called the Yale School made a big impact on the present generation of theological ethicists and biblical exegetes. The principal advocates of this approach – Brevard Childs and George Lindbeck as well as Hans Frei – emphasised in Wittgensteinian fashion the wisdom of situating biblical texts in the ritual and cultural-linguistic settings in which they were written and constructed as 'Scripture' or 'canon' and in which they have subsequently been read, rehearsed and interpreted. On this approach Scripture functions not in the precise literal-propositional terms in which Enlightenment critics of Scripture tend to read it (as also did the fundamentalists who responded to their criticism), but as a culture-shaping, character-forming genre which forms part of the larger set of processes and rituals that together construct moral communities of the kind Christians inhabit.

Story and narrative in this perspective take on a paradigmatic hermeneutical significance such that the particular narratives of Scripture are to be read in the context of a larger narrative history of creation and redemption of the kind Barth unfolds in the *Church Dogmatics*. And this larger narrative forms the setting in which the people of God are Sunday by Sunday formed and shaped as individuals and as a community who follow the non-violent redemptive way of the Son of God in a far country. That far country still exists, and it is still a place of struggle between the forces of light and darkness, between the reign of God and the alien powers who put to death the Son who came into exile. The powers remain, restrained but real, even after their triumphant defeat in the events of Christ's death and resurrection. And so preachers speak to their people as though they are returning week by week from exile to home, or from a field of

---

3   Hans Frei, *The Eclipse of Biblical Narrative: A Study in Eighteenth and Nineteenth Century Hermeneutics* (New Haven, CT: Yale University Press, 1980); Richard John Neuhaus, *The Naked Public Square: Religion and Democracy in America* (Grand Rapids, MI: Eerdmans, 1984).

battle to a community of peacemakers. At home in the sanctuary, singing the praises of their maker and redeemer, Christians celebrate who they really are by making peace and breaking bread. And they recall how it is that, throughout the millennia since Christ, their being Church in doing this has again and again turned the world upside down and challenged the powers that still claim to rule the world.

The preacher in the modern world, in the world *after* Christendom, stands in the place of an exilic prophet, seeking the welfare of the city in which the people find themselves resident but alien. And like the prophets she is called to juxtapose the divine Word of God and the social reality of exile in the midst of which Christians gather around Word and Sacrament where the Church is most real. And the preacher on this account exercises her vocation to form the Church around the contrast between the divine way, as described in Scripture, the way home, and the world as the place of exile.

This contrast between home and exile recalls the fact that the Church lives and witnesses in the midst of a world where the powers, though fallen and defeated, continue to attempt to assert their hold over human history, over the other creatures of God's creation, and at times over the Church as well. And hence the Church has not always lived up to her great calling. But as empires have risen and fallen, as dynasties have collapsed and wars have sundered the peace of the earth, the Church remains within history as the paradigm of a new world, a 'new creation', that God is bringing into being and that takes shape in institutions, practices and visions enacted before and in a watching world.

Christ challenged and defeated the powers not by military campaigns or political alliances but by performing the new world of the reign of God in inclusive feasts, healing miracles and exorcisms. And Christ resisted Rome, and the collaborators with Rome in first-century Palestine, by the weak speech of non-violent preaching. The first sermon Christ preached in Capernaum announced the acceptable year of the Lord – a reference to the biblical Jubilee year as described in Leviticus 25, in which all debts were written off, land reverted to its original owners, and bonded labourers and slaves were set free. Freedom from bondage to the power of debt and the violent coercion of slavery are the first words with which Christ challenges the reign of the powers. And this sermon in Capernaum is the paradigm for all subsequent preachers.

St Peter calls the Church into being on the day of Pentecost by preaching to Jew and Gentile in Jerusalem. St Paul turns from violently persecuting the Church to preaching peace between Jew and Gentile and so births the Church universal. Preaching is the definitive form of speech in which the Church is continuously called into existence from a world still under the sway of the powers. As Charles Campbell argues in *The Word Before the Powers*, preaching remains the definitive way of non-violent resistance to the powers, and hence the definitive form of Christian political speech, or public theology.[4]

On this account a crucial task of the preacher – and it is a political and prophetic task – is to name the powers that rule the world, to not cease from describing the insidious ways in which they tempt the people of God into coming under their influence while also remembering their defeat in the cross and resurrection of Christ. Naming the powers requires redescription of the world in ways that challenge the dominant descriptions in the horizons of the daily news, and of liberal progressive or putatively 'conservative' commentary (putative because conservatives who conserve either traditions or ecosystems from the destructiveness of money power are rare indeed). And hence the first act in many of the sermons which follow is precisely a focus on a particular political event or practice in which its popular presentation is challenged, and a new prophetic reading is developed in the light of Scripture and tradition.

The second act is to describe the resistant practices of the saints in which the defeat of the powers is already being performed and realised. Core congregational practices enacted Sunday by Sunday – such as almsgiving, Scripture reading, intercession, and

---

4   Charles Campbell, *The Word Before the Powers: An Ethic of Preaching* (Louisville, KY: Westminster John Knox Press, 2002).

Eucharistic feasting – are named and celebrated as practices which resist the control of money and sustenance by earthly powers. And practices that connect Christian worship with the everyday witness of the people of God in the world – growing and sharing food, fair trade, political engagement with the powers – are named and their meaning deepened.

The sermons in this book were all preached in the first decade of the third millennium since the birth of Christ. At no time in the last two thousand years has the rule of the powers been more totalising in their global reach, and more destructive of the peace of creation, than they have been in the present decade. There is hardly a square metre of ocean, or a farmed field, or a portion of the atmosphere, and there remain precious few forests, where the extractive and polluting hand of the global industrial economy is not evident. Topsoil is washed from the hills and valleys at an unprecedented rate; species are pressed to extinction as at no time in human history; the atmosphere is burdened with fossil fuel emissions; the sea is polluted with plastics and other chemicals and fished to near desert by industrial deep trawlers; forests are degraded to monocrop plantations; grasslands where animals grazed but a few years before turn to desert; and as the oceans acidify and warm, storms and droughts strengthen, and hunger increases among subsistence farmers and the landless. And yet the developed nations continue to export arms to the developing nations as if violence is their only redemption from the civil wars that accompany the deepening ecological crises of Africa and parts of Asia and the Americas. At the same time developed nations erect stronger fences and barriers against the millions of refugees from the extraction-driven storm of climate change and resource depletion that bears down on the small farms and communal forests of the South.

In the midst of the joint crises of war and growing hunger the world suffered two great human shocks, and a number of smaller ecological shocks in the first decade of the third millennium. One was a terrorist attack on the symbolic epicentre of the global extractive economy – the World Trade Center in New York City. The other was a near global financial collapse in which first

Northern Rock, then Lehmann Brothers, and then many other large banks and investment houses collapsed and were temporarily shored up with government money garnered from public taxes. But neither of these catastrophic signs led the powers that be to abandon the making and use of indiscriminate weapons or the coercive resource extraction that drives the poor into exile in polluted favellas and slums where resentment and violence breed. While prophetic voices linked the violence of the terrorists with the violence of an imperial industrial economy, these voices were drowned out by the call to avenge the deaths of North Americans through indiscriminate wars whose carnage continues in Muslim lands.

The ecological shocks of the last ten years included unprecedented melting of Arctic ice; strengthening tropical storms that created homelessness on a vast scale in Bangladesh, and on a smaller scale in New Orleans; excessive heat that dried wells and killed animals and people in North India and Tanzania, Paris and Chicago, and that caused small towns and farms to be engulfed in fire storms in California and Australia; extreme flooding that collapsed dams and drowned crops and city centres from the Rhine Valley and Rotheram in Europe to Kuala Lumpur and Choon King in Asia. And again, like the human signs of deep disturbance, the natural signs were ignored. Talk of change became more dominant. But practices to match the talk were drowned out by the clamour in the corporately owned media to return to the growth-fuelled, greed-driven consumptive economy that drives up greenhouse gas emissions just as it fuels financial and ecological debt and instability.

It is not hard in these events to see the hand of what Scripture calls the powers, or even of the judgment of God and of creation upon their misrule. It is however one thing to name the powers, and another to resist them and enact a different way. Encouraging, educating and forming the people of God in that way is the calling of the preacher in the third millennium just as it was in the first. All around there are seeds of hope in which the dominating powers are resisted. These seeds are in the Church and they are in the world. Those who plant and water them are nourished by a different vision of human flourishing than the one purveyed by advertisers of consumer goods and advocates of globalisation. In this alternative vision the prophetic contrast between what is and what might be takes flesh, and dwells. The preacher has the privilege of identifying the seeds of hope amidst the wreckage, and of setting forth through the words of Scripture, and in interaction with the practices of the people of God, a vision of salvation shaped by the Hebrew prophets, and by the form of the reign of God revealed in Jesus Christ the Incarnate Word. This vision is not constructed by choices made in a shopping mall or sustained in a well-guarded suburban house that is completely lacking in real resilience to the shocks that are coming if the powers do not abandon their current trajectory. It is the gift of God, the longing of all creatures, the desire of the nations. And again and again it is revealed to the people of God anew in the proclamation of the Word and in the breaking of bread.

Michaelmas, 2009

Advent

1. States of Alert

December 2004

And when you hear of wars and rumours of wars, do not be alarmed; this must take place, but the end is not yet. For nation will rise against nation, and kingdom against kingdom; there will be earthquakes in various places, there will be famines; this is but the beginning of the birth-pang.

Mark 13:7–8

When my students have gone home for their holidays – which they soon will do – I tend to leave my office on the Mound and head instead along George IV Bridge for the National Library of Scotland. In the last couple of years I have often been struck by the sign headed 'state of alert' at reception which tells me how worried the government is that day, or how worried it wants me to be. Like the Christian liturgical year the government also uses colour to alert us to different judgments of the times. Mostly it has been black recently but when it gets towards pink the library stewards start searching your laptop bag before you can go up to the reading room.

Government advertisements and signs in public buildings measuring the state of alert by different colours stoke a climate of fear. Rituals like having your bag searched on entering a public building, or taking off your shoes before boarding a plane also act as constant fear stokers – in the Bible Moses takes off his shoes in awe at the presence of Yahweh manifested in the burning bush, but in George Bush's America people take off their shoes for Bush!

The Gospel of Mark paints a vivid picture of world-shaking terror. Its message in drawing on the apocalyptic language of the day has some of the same apocalyptic tenor as the language of the war on terror:

*And when you hear of wars and rumours of wars, do not be
alarmed; this must take place, but the end is not yet. For
nation will rise against nation, and kingdom against kingdom;
there will be earthquakes in various places, there will be
famines; this is but the beginning of the birth-pangs ... In
those days, after that suffering, the sun will be darkened, and
the moon will not give its light, and the stars will be falling
from heaven, and the powers in the heavens will be shaken.
Then they will see 'the Son of Man coming in clouds' with
great power and glory.*

Mark 13:7–10

Christ affirms in his apocalypse much of what the ancients
already believed – that above the material and sensible world lies
another realm whose harmony and order are the source of all
true justice and peace. Thus the Son of Man comes 'on the
clouds' as he brings down to earth the order which is already
established in the sublunary clouds and the superlunary realm of
the stars. We can hear this same note in today's reading from
Isaiah:

*O that you would tear open the heavens and come down, so
that the mountains would quake at your presence – as when
fire kindles brushwood and the fire causes water to boil – to
make your name known to your adversaries, so that the nations
might tremble at your presence!*

Isaiah 64:1–2

Apocalyptic affirms that one day soon the invisible world will
break into the existing order in a definitive way and a new heaven
and a new earth will be created as Isaiah prophecies. A new
proximity between the order of the heavens and the order of the
earth will follow. And the forces of disorder and evil in the world
will be dethroned and 'all flesh will come to worship before the
Lord'.

But there is also a profoundly new note in Jesus' announce-
ment that the end is near and that history is moving towards its

fulfilment. The new age which he announces is already dawning in his ministry on earth, and this ministry does not take the form of war with the powers which usurp the reign of God on earth and persecute the faithful. Instead we see a radical recasting of apocalyptic categories. In the reign of God, which is already breaking in through Christ's ministry and teaching, power and violence are not so much overcome with force as subverted by humility and love. The beggar is welcomed into heaven while the careless wealthy man burns in hell, the despised publican is honoured and forgiven instead of the 'righteous' Pharisee, the labourers in the vineyard are given charge of land belonging to a greedy absentee landlord, a desperate and persistent widow receives mercy from a judge, a peasant farmer is miraculously able to find the land and seed he needs to grow a good crop.

Jesus was no apocalyptic prophet anxiously awaiting the end of the world and stoking revolutionary violence against corrupt kings and all-powerful emperors. On the contrary he affirms that the order of heaven has already broken through into the order of earth, and no power on earth can overcome the patient and trusting love of God's chosen ones.

But the early Christians were left, you might say, in the lurch after the Ascension of Christ. The new order was indeed breaking in to the reality of their lives together. But the world was hostile to this new order and they were harshly persecuted, by pagans and Jews as we already see evidenced in the book of Acts. It was in this situation that early Christian apocalyptic literature arose to sustain the first Christians as they suffered from persecution. It held before them the reward they would ultimately receive for their fidelity in suffering and it affirmed that the reign of justice was already breaking through in the liturgy of word and sacrament.

Whereas Christian apocalyptic calls Christians to watch and pray so that the kingdom which God has already inaugurated may break in among them, the terrorist and the war-monger both believe that it is up to them to halt the evil horde and to attempt to direct history's outcome. The language of a 'war on terror' over-determines history – it announces in apocalyptic terms that those who are not with us are against us and that 'evil is real' and can only be resisted by equivalent and even stronger evil and violence.

Advent is the Christian 'state of alert'; its colour is purple, not red. And it trains us not to fear 'the terror of the night nor the arrow that flies by day' but instead to wait patiently for the coming of the Lord.

For Gregory the Great, who first established the pattern of Four Sundays of Advent for the Western Church, the principal focus of the season was on preparation for the Feast of the Incarnation. In the Middle Ages, provoked by corruption in God's Holy Church, a new revolutionary emphasis on the Second Coming shifted the focus of Christian apocalyptic from the Incarnation to the Second Coming. And many conservative Christians today embrace this same revived millenarianism, and neglect the original meaning of Advent – that in Christ's first coming the world as we now know it is already being redeemed.

But against those who look for the end of the world in apocalyptic violence, or those who foolishly imagine they can bring peace or security through apocalyptic and indiscriminate warfare the Advent hope is that the peace which comes from above is the only true peace. And it is first and foremost the work of God.

This hope, first announced by angels to shepherds, means that despite appearances men of violence are no longer in control of history; after Christ Christians learn from apocalyptic that those who would seek to determine history's outcome through violence will never succeed. For the end of all times, and of all our lives, is revealed in the new beginning which is God's coming as Emmanuel, the Lord of heaven who becomes a child of earth.

When the angels announce the coming of Christ to the shepherds their first words are 'fear not'. Christ also teaches his disciples, in the words which precede today's gospel, not to fear when they are brought before the authorities to testify on Christ's behalf for the Holy Spirit will teach them what to say. Our Advent state of alert does not require us to be fearful but expectant, faithful, watchful – the Lord has come, and his reign is a reign of peace. And the peace Christ made on the cross means we can love our enemies – we need no longer fear what they can do to us.

Against those who interpret our Gospel today as predicting that history will literally end in violence before Christ can come again, and that it may even be the duty of those who can to seek to bring about this violent end, the true apocalyptic recalls the words of Christ 'blessed are the peacemakers' and 'love your enemies, and pray for them that persecute you'. The Christian 'state of alert' requires us to be suspicious of political messiahs and of their perverse paths to peace. It involves us in reading the stories of our times through the story which begins at the Annunciation and ends at the Ascension. In this story empires tremble, the rich are humbled, violence is undone but not by might nor by power but by the divine Spirit who inhabits and inspires the reign of the Prince of Peace.

Christ in his coming fulfils the desire of the nations because his reign brings down the perfect and unchanging justice from above to the imperfect and fallen world here below and so the longing for wholeness which the order of the heavens provokes is at last fulfilled:

> O Come desire of the nations, Show
> Thy kingly reign on earth below
> Thou cornerstone uniting all
> Restore the ruin of our fall
> O Come O Come Emmanuel.

2. Creating Hunger and Growing Food

December 2008

He has filled the hungry with good things.

Luke 1:53

Two weeks ago my daughter lamented at dinner that a tin of tomatoes had cost her 98 pence at a local store, which was double the price it would have been a few months previously. The government's Chief Scientific Adviser, Professor John Beddington, announced recently that food prices will remain high both in the UK and around the world for the foreseeable future. He blamed the growth of world population, which is presently rising at six million a month. However the authors of a significant investigation in the Washington Post blame city speculators for rising commodity prices. In recent months they have piled out of dubious hedge funds and banks exposed to the sub-prime mortgage crisis and into futures trading in real commodities including cereals, copper, gold and oil. The price of oil doubled in little more than a year and since oil plays such a large role in the present food production and supply system this has inevitably inflated food prices with the rising costs of oil-derived fertilisers, pesticides, and tractor and truck fuels. Global warming, caused largely by the burning of oil, has also played a role in rising food prices. More than two billion people still live directly from what they grow and many are finding climatic changes are challenging their ability to grow enough food to sustain for their families. And to make matters worse governments and corporations have decided that one way to free themselves from Middle Eastern oil, while appearing to be 'green', is to make gasoline from food crops such as corn and palm oil instead of drilling it from the ground. Scientific investigation reveals that biofuels actually have a larger carbon footprint than Middle Eastern oil, but this has not put an end to the project. And the resultant diversion of a proportion of food crops to fuelling private cars has acted as one more spur to rising food prices.

At the birth of modern capitalism economists, politicians and traders blamed the poor for the famines that spread in its imperial wake. But these wealthy commentators lived in cities that expropriated and stockpiled the stolen product of the labour and lands of the poor. Millions went hungry and tens of thousands died in the Irish potato famines although there was plenty of food available in the houses of the rich in Dublin and in storehouses in England. Professor Beddington too is blaming the poor. And he is not alone. As in the nineteenth century, the world is again governed by free market liberals of left and right, Tory and Labour, Republican and Democrat, bureaucrat and plutocrat, who believe that when markets and money rule, unfettered by the demands of justice, freedom reigns. According to the neoliberals those who deserve to live well will be empowered by a global free market so to do while the feckless, such as those who have too many children without sufficient means to feed them, will suffer and so learn the error of their ways.

Now I agree with Professor Beddington that there are too many babies being born. But what prevents the poor from having smaller families is the theft of their patrimony by the rigged markets imposed on their lands and governments by the financial corporations and institutions of the West. As condition for repaying foreign debt developing countries have abolished agricultural protection for small farmers, turned vast areas of land over to corporate agriculture for cash crops for export to the North, and sold off their government stores of surplus and seed which tradition had trained them to set aside for bad times. Malawi, one of the best-governed countries in Africa, needed food aid in 2006 for precisely these reasons. And yet farm protection and surplus storage continue in Europe and North America as permitted under the unfair rules of the World Trade

Organization. And hence the eventual failure of the Doha trade round in Geneva, much lamented by neoliberals such as Peter Mandelson and Gordon Brown. But this failure turned on the systemic injustices which characterise global trade in agricultural and other commodities and in particular the requirement by North America and Europe that they should be able to continue subsidising their farmers, protecting them with tariffs, and dumping subsidised foods on developing country markets, while developing countries should not subsidise or protect their farmers in any way. Despite the failure of Doha Peter Mandelson is still trying to persuade individual African countries to sign up to Economic Partnership Agreements with Europe which require them not to discriminate in any way between domestic and overseas businesses. The government of Senegal under this arrangement will have to continue to allow European trawlers to fish out its waters and cause penury amongst its fishing communities, and to permit the import of subsidised European chicken, chicken feed and tomatoes and so ruin the livelihoods of local farmers. According to Traidcraft, Britain's first and largest Fair Trade company, Europe uses underhand and bullying tactics in trying to foist these unjust deals on its former colonies and their clear consequence – if they are signed – will be the continuing under-development of the countries that sign them.

Africans and many Asians and Latin Americans continue to have what Professor Beddington and others would say is too many children. But this is because they lack education in and access to family planning techniques; because many of the children they have will die from hunger and preventable diseases; and because the only guarantee they have of living into old age themselves is to have enough children to work their lands and so feed them when they can no longer do this themselves. The core reason that these are continuing blights on the lives of the poor are the very neoliberal policies over which the government Professor Beddington advises presides in its relations with the developing world, and with the less than wealthy in its own backyard. Thus many poor people around the world are forced to pay user charges to send their children to school, or to attend primary health care clinics because the International Monetary Fund and the World Bank require such charges as condition for foreign debt relief and rescheduling arrangements. Neoliberals do not believe that any government service should be provided without charge because only when price is affixed to services can the service be sold off and privatised and so returned from public provision to the superior 'efficiency' of the market. It is the same neoliberal policy that has seen the rise of user charges and privatisation in the National Health Service and in Higher Education, with a correlative decline in the take-up of charged-for services by the poor even in Britain.

A few years ago, at a conference on food and trade in St George's House, Windsor, I put it to a senior civil servant that the answer to the growing disconnect between the lives of the not so wealthy and good quality food in Britain and else-where – now made much worse by rising food prices – was the lack of connection between the people and the land, a connection which in Britain has been sundered longer than in any other country. He almost choked on our very nice dinner and said that this was pure romanticism. There is no going back. The future is in 'free' trade, not in local and sustainable foods.

I thought he was wrong then and I still do. The word culture comes from agriculture. Culture grows rich and well in communities that grow food. The mass culture of Britain is in meltdown as it is in the United States. And the reason is the disconnect between people and production which corporations have prosecuted and sustained for the last hundred years as they have abolished the jobs of working people, first from fields and forests and now from factories and workshops. These jobs have been exported to developing countries where trade unions are frequently outlawed or have never developed, where wages are very much lower and where environmental regulations are lax or non-existent. As is well known, many of these jobs take the form of sweatshop labour which is often coercive and in some cases is effectively bonded labour. More than a hundred years of legislation and regulation of the workplace has outlawed such working conditions in Europe and North America but corporations simply recreate the pollution and poverty wages that were once typical in Victorian and Edwardian cities in the developing world. We urgently need to recover a local food economy and a local economy of making if we are to rescue this country from its civilisational decline, while also reducing our unsustainable dependency on the carbon intensity of globally sourced foods and other commodities.

I was in Rome in the summer – a city in a country where the family, family businesses, and the culture of food, remain strong – and I saw no drunkenness in the streets. Some of us will have seen on television Jamie Oliver visiting Italian schools and seeing local women preparing a simple but high-quality dish of pasta for the children in the school every day, which every child in the school eats. And as he pointed out, food that is grown and prepared locally is a far cry from the fatty factory-farmed food prepared in many British educational establishments.

Thomas Merton, in the first volume of his journal, reflects on the contrast between Sunday afternoons in France and in England. He observes how in England there was a sense of *ennui* and listlessness on a Sunday afternoon in the 1930s characterised by long listless walks and chunks of doughy bread for tea. But in France, to the contrary, Sunday 'was always a feast'.[5] The difference was not that shops were open in France but that the food, and the joyful and lengthy gathering around the food, set an appropriate note of festivity for the enduring religious custom of rest from work. In France today there remains a local food culture so that even motorway service cafés as well as many restaurants take pride in serving up local dishes, and hypermarkets endeavour to stock local produce sourced from local farmers. But when a large new branch of Sainsbury's opened in Edinburgh in the early 1990s and I went along they only had English produce. I wrote and protested to the Sainsbury HQ. The careful answer I received from the company's headquarters was that all of the fresh food in Sainsbury's was gathered and prepared in one large factory in North Wales so it did not matter where it was sourced.

---

5   Thomas Merton, *Run to the Mountain: The Story of Vocation*, ed. Patrick Hart (New York: HarperCollins, 1996), 32.

It is not only the transportation footprint of such a system of food marketing that is unsustainable. Equally destructive is the loss of connection between people in cities and the farming communities that surround the cities on which farmers endeavour to grow food in the face of the monopolistic power, and unfair pricing regimen, of the four big supermarket chains. Farmers receive less than ten per cent of the money value at which their food is sold but just fifty years ago they received half of the value. Consequently farmers large and small are getting out of farming and land is bought up by the supermarkets and their suppliers for contract farming, which is reliant on temporary migrant labour and corporate farm managers.

There is plenty of land and plenty of rain to water the soil in Britain. But too much of this land belongs to too few people. As Hilaire Belloc argues in his classic essay *The Servile State*, the influence of Christianity over 800 years in these islands was such that in the course of time those who had known feudal serfdom and servitude for hundreds of years began to enjoy a lessening of the burden of the onerous nature of feudal dues, and a growth in respect from their feudal masters.[6] Belloc argues that it was Catholic Christianity's concept of the dignity and freedom of the person before God that created – throughout Catholic Europe – a situation in which rulers began to respect the ruled, and labourers and serfs gradually became self-sufficient peasant farmers. Hence by the thirteenth century the land of Britain was distributed in such a way that most households could provision themselves in only ten weeks of agricultural labour, while they owed a lesser proportion of their time to the church or the local lord which could be given in the form of crops or labour.

Belloc argues that the event that crushed this peasant self-sufficiency was the Tudor dissolution of the monasteries which took over a quarter of the land of England – that had been left in trust to the Church – and gave it to the barons and lords who attended the Court and sat in the Parliament in Westminster. And these newly enriched barons and lords in subsequent centuries

---

6   Hilaire Belloc, *The Servile State* (London: T. N. Foulis, 1912).

used the English parliament to write a number of Acts of Enclosure under which they stole even more of the land – in the form of common land and peasant farms – from the people than Henry VIII did at the Reformation. The one royal theft, orchestrated by Thomas Cromwell and Cranmer, led in time to thousands of other thefts and so England was the first truly modern industrial country – not because Newcomen invented the steam engine and Watt perfected it, but because the Tudors and their baronial heirs created the first landless peasant class who were disposed through their landlessness to take up miserable wage-labour in mills and factories that was offered them instead of the workhouse. Now that much of the industry has gone the descendants of the landless are even more bereft since they have neither means of growing food nor regular industrial work, and live either from state handouts – as do many more millions than official unemployment statistics reveal – or in fear of losing their jobs in the current recession.

The Scottish Parliament in one of its greatest acts inaugurated a bill in 2001, known as the Land Reform (Scotland) Act 2003. The Act was designed to do something about rural landlessness and established a community right to buy land in Scottish law. And so far the Land Reform Commission established under the Act has supported households on the Isle of Gigha and in parts of the Highlands in buying the freehold of the land on which they live from large landowners so that they might again grow their own food and fuel and in the process repopulate lands devastated by the blight of absentee owners and the sporting estate. I heard recently of a group of people in a town in the central belt attempting to use the Act for a similar purpose. Whereas in England and Wales the millions of people who are on waiting lists for allotments that cities are unable to provide have no remedy other than to wait, the Land Reform Act in Scotland makes another way possible. And Christians, through the Land Reform Convention which met periodically in the 1990s, were active in pressing for this new law.

I have recently, after a gap of thirty years, begun growing some of my own food again and I have been amazed to find how sensually and spiritually rewarding digging the soil and pulling food out of it are. A meal eaten from freshly picked food with family and friends is a foretaste of heaven. A tin of tomatoes doubling in price is the taste of the hell we make when we forget the created gift of good earth. This giftedness is celebrated every Sunday in the Christian Eucharist which is the feast that transforms food and drink into true communion among and between God and the people of God. And it is celebrated on ordinary days by those who grow and eat their own food. This should not be a privilege but the patrimony of every human being. Then we, and the hungry, may be delivered from the merciless trades of speculators by the good things the earth has given and human hands have made.

Christmas

3. Simeon and the Clone

December 2007

Lord, now lettest thou thy servant depart in peace, according to thy word:
For mine eyes have seen thy salvation,
Which thou hast prepared before the face of all people;
A light to lighten the Gentiles, and the glory of thy people Israel.

Luke 2:30–32

A religious group called the Raelians, who believe that human life was begun by aliens, claimed recently that it had won a bizarre clandestine race to produce a human clone. Their leader said a baby girl was born from an egg fertilised by a skin cell from her mother. Dr Brigitte Boisselier, who calls herself bishop of the Raelians, offered no proof to back her claim at a press conference in Florida, but said an independent panel of scientists would be allowed to verify it with DNA tests in the next eight or nine days. The Raelian movement was begun by a French sports commentator, Claude Vorilhon, in 1973 after he claimed to have met aliens in a spaceship at the extinct volcano overlooking Clermont Ferand. The aliens told him that they – the Elohim – were the creators of human beings 10,000 years ago through the science of genetics and cell manipulation. The Raelians believe that by developing this technology they will find the key to immortality because the aliens became immortal through the same technology.

The technique used in cloning, known as nuclear transfer, was first developed in Edinburgh by Scottish scientist Ian Wilmut in the production of Dolly the sheep. DNA is transferred into an embryo through a needle thinner than a human hair, and successfully fertilised embryos may then be transferred into the womb. The technique is very unreliable and for every regenerated embryo, hundreds are not viable. But a small number of cloned sheep, and many hundreds of cloned mice, have already been born and viable cloned embryos, using human DNA and the outer 'sack' of an embryo taken from a cow, have been produced in a laboratory in Massachusetts.

When it was first developed, most scientists said that nuclear transfer technology should not be used for human cloning. Now Wilmut, and many of his colleagues in the cloning race, support human cloning. Some, including Wilmut, want to limit the technique to medical cloning. The idea is that couples with a history of serious genetic disorders, such as cystic fibrosis, submit their sperm and embryos to test-tube embryo fertilisation. Scientists would take a successfully fertilised embryo, remove the defective gene which causes the genetic condition, and clone the genetically cleaned-up embryo. The cloned embryo would then be implanted in the mother who would give birth to a cloned child which in every respect, but for the disease-inducing gene, would be identical to her original embryo.

Human cloning would in theory allow the engineering of test-tube babies whose genetic inheritance would be unparalleled in the history of human evolution. Propensities to diseases with a known genetic component – such as heart disease – could be removed. At the same time scientists could genetically enhance physical and even mental characteristics such as intelligence, eyesight and height. Even personality traits, like a propensity to addictive behaviour, could in theory be corrected. The result would be the creation of 'designer babies', and ultimately of a new race of genetically superior humans. In the high-tech labs of the bioengineers the twentieth-century idea of eugenics, which came closest to reality in the racial engineering and genocide of Hitler's evil Third Reich, may finally be realised. Instead of a master race, the new eugenics could produce a superclass of genetically enhanced human beings whose superiority would be designed by scientists and parents wealthy enough to pay for the technology to clone themselves, their embryos or their children.

The declared intention of promoters of the new eugenics is to improve the human condition and reduce suffering and disease, and in the case of the Raelians, even to cheat death itself. But if the Raelians believe in aliens who cloned humans and that through cloning technology humans will achieve alien-like immortality, as Christians we have a uniquely material and bodily vision of salvation from human failings, and from disease and death, a vision which is revealed in the birth of the child Jesus to Mary and Joseph from Nazareth. Christians see life in the body not as an encumbrance to be technologically mastered or overcome but as a preparation for a good death, and they see life in the body of the child Jesus as the preparation for Christ's saving death on the cross. Ever since the resurrection of Christ from that saving death, Christians have seen physical death as a transformation of identity – both body and soul – into a life of intimate union and joyful praise of God which is made possible in the resurrection of Jesus who is 'the first born of the dead'.

Today's Gospel is a vivid example of this faith for in it we see the old priest Simeon declaring that now he is ready to 'depart in peace' because at last he has seen with his own eyes the promised Messiah who will bring salvation to Gentiles and for Jews. And the prophet Anna similarly announces that this child is the chosen one. Like the Magi and the shepherds, Anna and Simeon are witnesses to the truth that God has come to redeem God's people, not as an alien or as a clone of Moses or of a god-king but as a vulnerable child born to ordinary parents in a distant outpost of the Roman Empire.

The scientific quest for genetically engineered human perfection, and for deferred death through cloned organ transplants, is a manifestation of the modern fear of death in a society where resurrection is no longer believed in and where aging bodies, even mortality itself, are seen as problems for science to fix. But the irony is that as we devote our best minds and considerable resources to extending the physical limits of human existence for the privileged few, the lives of at least a billion people are still blighted by preventable poverty and environmental catastrophe. The values, wealth and technology which are bringing about the new eugenics are the same as those which are placing such severe strain on the physical limits of the life-support systems of the planet.

Many who no longer practise Christianity, and even some who do, increasingly substitute belief in reincarnation for belief in resurrection. But whichever we believe, both doctrines involve the idea that our personal identity and our present bodily existence are not identical. Both acknowledge limits to bodily existence. And both indicate that human happiness is to be found not by denying these limits but by acknowledging them, and by restraining obsessive desires for material wealth or bodily perfection, and even longevity. Resisting these limits in a quest for wealth and technologies which together can create new cloned children, or even cloned organs, will not save us or our children from death – it certainly won't make us immortal. But owning that there are limits to what we should do with technology just might help to save the planet, as well as our genetic inheritance, in their flawed but still wondrous diversity, for our children's children.

The child who is born in Bethlehem and raised in Nazareth remains the light of the Gentiles and the hope of Israel. He is the source of our hope of redemption in the body. It is not that this redemption does not have an outworking in the material improvement of life on earth. Far from it. The conditions in which the people of God were living in first-century Palestine were increasingly characterised by debt, slavery, hunger, and foreign oppression, as witnessed by the near-refugee status of his parents at the time of his birth. But the history of the worship of the Christ child has proven a mystic key to human life on earth. Through this key the powers which seek to bind human history are judged, slaves have been redeemed, and the hungry are fed.

The Raelians worship the wrong god. But so too do those who seek to manufacture babies instead of receiving them, natural born, as the divine blessing on the union of two human beings in mutual love. And yet Christ is not born from such a union but by the mysterious union of a virgin with the divine Spirit. Here is the great paradox of Christmas. We celebrate in the darkness of

winter the coming into the world of a birth that has not been
before, nor ever will be again. This non-repeatable event is the
incarnate dwelling of God in the womb of Mary. In the darkness
of sin appears the star of redemption. In the light of this event God
creates the world again. In this light, salvation from death and sin
is revealed not as the work of humans but the gift of God. Our
salvation is to receive this gift, and in receiving it we receive back
our own life, not by our own making but as divinely given.

In the birth of the Christ child judgment is declared on our
civilisation's attempts to remake our genetic inheritance by
technological control, just as it was declared on the leaders of the
Jews who sought to control the destiny of the people of God by
consorting with alien powers. For Christ who is our life is
begotten not made.[7] He was in the beginning with God, he was
with God from before the dawn of time, and not made for the
first time in the womb of Mary. And so in devoting ourselves
anew this Christmas to worship the Christ child we do not give
ourselves to a plan of our own making or to a political messiah;
no. We give ourselves to the source of all that is, who knew you
and me before any eye had seen us in our mother's womb, and
who is present to each of us now as we share in the breaking of
the bread.

---

7   See further Oliver O'Donovan, *Begotten or Made? Human Procreation and Medical Technique* (Oxford: Oxford
University Press, 1984).

Epiphany

4. The Return of the King

January 2003

And when they were come into the house, they saw the young child with Mary his mother, and fell down, and worshipped him: and when they had opened their treasures, they presented unto him gifts; gold, and frankincense, and myrrh.

Matthew 2:11

I enjoyed Peter Jackson's last film in the *Lord of the Rings* trilogy – *The Return of the King* – but I also found it disappointing. The great battle and the ring's journey up the mountain into the lake of fire are all there and are superbly done but in the book there is more than a battle won by valiant and courageous men, more than a journey up the mountain and a struggle at the top, and there is more at stake than force of arms. What is missing from the film is more telling than what is in it. In the book the triumph of good over evil is not simply down to a battle won, a beloved obsession with the ring given up. For when brave Hobbits return to the Shire there is the scouring of the shire. Evil is still at large, it has wrought its effects even on the peaceable people of the Shire with their stylish arts and crafts holes in the hills – the wrong people are running the show, schools and hospitals sold to the highest bidders, the bouncers and the bandits have taken power, and wealth is piled up through greed and theft – the virtues of a Frodo or a Bilbo Baggins, the weapons of the weak, are cast aside. Reversing all of this is no easy task and the scouring is a time of reckoning, of judgment, of evil trounced and enemies reconciled. The one big victory calls forth a thousand smaller struggles and only those who learn that victory is not to the strong, and true power not to the mighty, win through.

The infancy narratives of the New Testament are not like the film of *The Return of the King* but they are a lot more like Tolkien's original book. For in these narratives there is no suggestion that this infant king who was around at the beginning of time, this gentle metaphysical giant who is God in flesh incarnate, re-enters a world that welcomes him back. How does John have it? 'He came to his own and his own knew him not and the light shone in the darkness and the darkness could not overcome it' (John 1:11, 1:5) – though the implication is that it tried. For Matthew the metaphysical takes more of a back seat. But the message is the same: no sooner has the king returned to his creation than the powers who usurp creation's rule are struggling over him. The oriental potentates come to worship him as the child king who will redeem the nations, while Caesar's vassal, King Herod, seeks to kill him as a threat to his own power. As a king tries to have Jesus killed the wise men who visit him from a far country bring gifts, such strange gifts which presage a life lived in the face of evil: gold – the metal of kingship; frankincense – the incense of holiness; and myrrh – the balm of suffering. And to protect the child King the kings deceive their kingly host and 'returned to their own country by another road'. Just like in a classic fairy story, evil is not defeated by unambiguous heroism.

The film *The Return of the King* is a modern take on the ancient story of the struggle between good and evil – in it good trounces evil and all but those who threw in their lot with the Dark Lord Sauron, and the forces of Mordor, live happily ever after. But the book is more like a traditional fairy story. Fairy stories are not as fashionable as they once were. They are full of such monsters – child-eating giants, pig-eating wolves, incestuous brothers and sisters, narcissistic witches – that modern political correctness often keeps them from our children's bedtimes. But like the story of Herod, who killed the innocents and drove the holy family into exile, they do not hide the true nature of things from small children – on the contrary their art is in presenting the full panoply of the human predicament in mythic form. Death, deviousness, deceit, demons – they are all there and the message is not that these things are easily defeated, or even that their defeat is always assured. No, the heroes and heroines of these stories suffer in their struggle with evil. But finally they help to uncover a better life, a truer good, a deeper fulfilment than the characters they struggle against. Evil does not pay, not because its end is always bloody but because in the end the greedy giant, the wicked sisters and the wicked witch, while acting out their evil fantasies, do not find happiness. But Jack and Cinderella and Snow White do; not because they live 'happily ever after' – children are not that easily taken in – but because unlike their wicked opponents they are able to form lasting and loving relationships.

As Bruno Bettelheim points out in his wonderful book *The Uses of Enchantment* the point about such stories is that they face the child with what the child already knows, but that his parents would hide from her – evil is not without its attractions and enchantments.[8] And evil is not just out there; it is inside each one of us. Against the grain of many modern children's stories, in fairy tales evil is as omnipresent as virtue. In practically every traditional fairy tale good and evil are given body in the form of heroines or heroes, monsters or tyrants just as good and evil are omnipresent in life and the propensities for both are present in every man. It is this duality which poses the moral problem, and requires the struggle to solve it. Children know that the struggle is within – they need to be assured that they can win but they will not do this if we hide it from them, pretend that goodness is always triumphant. Nor will they learn it if they absorb the message of the modern mythology of redemptive violence – that good wins over evil by knocking it for six, by terminating it or carpet bombing it.

In Washington Cathedral more than two years ago the self-styled Christian leader of the free world announced an intention to 'rid the world of evil'. This was a deeply troubling statement; for as one American commentator put it 'I can't even rid my own neighbourhood of evil', and as another said 'I can't rid my own heart of evil'.

---

8   Bruno Bettelheim, *The Uses of Enchantment: The Meaning and Importance of Fairy Tales* (London: Penguin, 1976).

'Evil is real', Bush also intoned. And here he made another crucial mistake. For Christians have always believed that evil is less real than goodness and this is why in the end goodness overcomes evil, not by good people adopting evil means, but by the attraction, the deeper, truer reality of goodness. But the intent to 'rid the world of evil' has mandated the adoption of evil means in the so-called 'war on terror' and this has led rapidly to America and Britain colluding in methods of punishment and revenge that have included indiscriminate attacks on civilian as well as military targets, the use of animal cages, hoods and chains to imprison men and boys on and off the battlefield, and the use of interrogation techniques on prisoners which are defined as torture and proscribed in the twentieth-century Geneva conventions on limiting evils in warfare.

Those who ascribe reality to evil are drawn to its power, like those who serve the Dark Lord of Mordor. They come to believe that smashing what they oppose requires the nihilistic sacrifice of the good, the true and the beautiful. And this nihilism is catching. No wonder that the Christmas number one hit (in the UK) this year was that extraordinarily beautiful and yet maudlin song from the soundtrack of the film *Donnie Darko* – 'It's a Mad World'. The song's pivotal line is 'the dreams in which I'm dying are the best I ever had'. Such nihilism is hardly redemptive. It's more Gollum than Gandalf.

And yet given the choice between 'Rudolf the Red Nosed Reindeer' and 'It's a Mad World', I know which I would choose. At least there is no pretence, no tinsel, in the second song. There *is* some pretty weird stuff going down, and the first Christmas did not put an end to death and evil, at least not in the sense of executing their author like an evil dictator before a kangaroo court. Indeed as we know *the* Return of the King actually ends with the death of the king and not the death of Herod. And this is not the ending the Israelites imagined, nor even the one Isaiah predicts. Where are the fawning nations when Jesus is on trial before Herod – not fawning but preparing his death in the form of the Gentile cross.

And Matthew is not inclined to hide the truth of this ending from us. He adds to Isaiah's Christmas gift list – frankincense and gold – the gift of myrrh and that is the gift which unlocks the real meaning of what the astrologers saw, for the Egyptians used it in embalming the dead. At the end of their journey the magi return to their own country, but as Eliot so wonderfully puts it they were 'no longer at ease' 'in the old dispensation'. They go back to their shires but there is no scouring – the people are still clutching their 'alien gods'. And so the magi still await the death in whose overcoming Christ will be revealed as the King of Jew and Gentile.

What of us? We live after that death and the resurrection also. Was this just once for all – a mythic struggle that had to be played out in the light of which all is changed? Well in one sense yes. But in another we still live in our places, in the shires, but we are not meant to find ease there for the people still clutch their gods and it is now we who are aliens – resident aliens in a world that has still not acknowledged that Christ is King; we are no longer at home in the old dispensation and so, as Eliot puts it, 'we shall not cease from exploration, and the end of all our exploring will be to arrive where we started and know the place for the first time.'

And how will we find it? Simplicity, spirituality, tongues of fire are Eliot's hints in *Little Gidding*. Christ does not leave us bereft – he too gives gifts and these are gifts which enable us to worship. Like the wise men we are all obsessive – we are creatures, we long to return to the source. And we find so many ways we think will lead us back, or at least fill the void. But we do best when we follow the astrologers' example – Jesus is the one who is to be our obsession, he is the one who can be light in our darkness. But we must create space for him, take time to attend to the flame, and allow ourselves to be drawn to the light. Worship, prayer, silent joyful adoration in the stillness of the morning before the sun is up or the buses running – these are the gifts we can offer for the return of the king. And they will make us, and him, glad.

Lent

5. Happiness and Faithfulness

March 2003

God said to Noah, 'This is a sign of the covenant which I have established between me and all flesh that is upon the earth.'

Genesis 9:17

The economist Richard Layard recently delivered three lectures in the London School of Economics on the results of a survey into happiness and wealth which revealed, to the surprise of many, that increased affluence in Britain and America, measured by such things as better homes, more clothes and cars, and foreign holidays, had not translated into a general increase in feelings of happiness or personal well-being. Layard also drew on a number of other surveys, which reveal for example that 29 per cent of women under 30 reported suffering problems with nerves or depression in 1990 compared to only 16 per cent in 1982, and that 43 per cent of children regularly suffer from anxiety or feel stressed.[9]

Modern politicians in Britain and America apparently believe that the road to the end of the rainbow is paved with gold: find the economic levers to provide individuals with more spending power, reduce taxation, make the labour market more mobile and advance economic growth and the result will be a collective rise in welfare, well-being or happiness. Layard's results though show that on the contrary marginal increases in affluence have little effect on the happiness of the comfortable, whereas poverty in the midst of affluence, and unemployment, are the two surest indicators of unhappiness. So if the politician wants to increase happiness the answer is to manage the economy for full employment and use taxes progressively to distribute income and wealth

---

9   See further Richard Layard, *Happiness: Lessons from a New Science* (London: Penguin, 2005).

more equitably. But so long as politicians and the media continue to promote individual selfishness and consumer satisfaction in the market as the means to increased well-being for all, they will inevitably achieve the opposite result – greater collective unhappiness and misery.

One particular aspect of this misery is that when people in Britain are asked the question 'do you think that most people can be trusted?' the proportion of trusters has fallen steadily from 56 per cent in 1959 to only 31 per cent in 1995. A similar decline in trust has occurred in the USA but *not* in Continental Europe. It would appear that as the US and the UK have promoted an individualistic, lower tax and privatised economy so the levels of both happiness and trust have fallen correlatively in both countries. In other words people feel less bad about pursuing their interests regardless of others, but as a result they trust others much less as well.

The story of Noah tells of an ancient society in which something similar seems to have happened. So selfish and untrustworthy had the general mass of humanity become that the book of Genesis tells that God sent a flood which killed almost all of them, though Noah and his family are saved, and they in turn save the species in the ark. And when the ark finally came to rest on Mount Ararat we can hardly imagine the feelings of trauma that Noah and his family must have had – no doubt the animals too – by the long tyranny of the waters over the land.

In response God makes an everlasting covenant of fertility and blessing with Noah and his descendants wherein God promises never to destroy life on such a scale again. And God makes the covenant not just with humans but with 'all flesh', with 'every living creature'. The covenant is sealed with the rainbow in the sky, which is the recurring sign that God will be faithful to the earth even were its inhabitants again to be as wicked and rebellious as they had been in the days of Noah. And God's covenant with Noah is no fraud – he does not send him on a mission to discover in the end that God is not truly God. The covenant God makes with God's people, despite their frequent testing of it, is one that God honours again and again.

We learn from the covenant something very fundamental about the nature of God, which is that God does not set up the world and just leave it to go its own way. This is a Creator who is in continuing relation to the creation. And even when the people fail to keep the covenant, God goes on declaring his intention to be faithful to them. This covenant-making Creator manifests this fidelity by calling a particular people and choosing to sustain them and remain bound to them and so to reveal the great and mysterious faithfulness of divine love. Fidelity is central in the biblical view of the love of God. And there is no real difference between God's love and God's faithfulness – love is faithful to the end.

How different this is to the modern understanding of love. Love in popular songs is more often described as a magical happening, and it is often a temporary one; love may be the 'sweetest thing' but it is also fickle, it moves on, people fall into it and they fall out of it. And it is not just relationships that are becomingly increasingly impermanent in the popular cult of love. Everything is becoming less permanent in our new extreme capitalist society. As George Orwell notes in his novel *Coming Up for Air*, 'there was a temporary feeling about everything', whereas people once had 'something that we haven't got now' – 'a feeling of security even when they weren't secure … a feeling of continuity.'[10]

The principal dissolver of bonds in our society is the economic market which works by a constant process of 'creative destruction'; as new technologies come on stream old jobs are destroyed, or corporations move them to places where 'labour' is cheaper. Companies amalgamate to maximise their profits by cornering the market. And so old loyalties are torn up, communities abandoned and workers fired. Adam Smith, the great sage of Kirkaldy, called this mercantilism. London's Karl Marx talked about this tendency of capitalism to destroy everything and remake it again as a condition in which 'all that is solid melts into air'. Neither thought it would redeem the nations.

---

10   George Orwell, *Coming Up for Air* (London: Victor Golancz, 1939), 138.

The greatest irony of the politics which has dominated Britain since 1979 is that although it was conservative in name it was revolutionary in nature. Faithfulness to local custom or tradition and loyalty to hallowed ways of doing things were both abandoned in favour of the engine of enterprise and the virtue of wealth creation – nothing was to get in the way of the magic of the market. But as Layard's work shows, two of the biggest causes of unhappiness in our society are unemployment and divorce. Both involve dissolution – of the bonds of work and the bonds of family. And as the market, and the associated consumer culture of 'me first', let rip these were precisely the social diseases which inexorably increased; we may now be collectively richer in monetary and material terms but we are a sadder, less trusting and less faithful society.

Impermanence is also a feature of consumer capitalism and the throw-away society and perhaps this is just one more reason why Britain is so far behind the rest of Europe in recycling and reusing natural resources. Floating on our oceans there are such large quantities of trash that ocean currents concentrate great vortexes of trash. And these form large masses of material. The largest is in the Pacific Ocean between the coast of California and Hawaii and the area it covers is the size of Texas. The plastic and other material gathered there originated on land, and was carried there from beaches, rivers and streams. Scientists have recently found that all this floating plastic actually begins to break down in the ocean water, as chemicals leach out of the plastic. And this means that the fish that we eat from the ocean are increasingly polluted with toxic chemicals.

Waste is a hazard also to ocean-dwelling mammals and large fish. Bits of white polystyrene floating in the water are easily mistaken for cuttlefish, and plastic bags for jellyfish, by those wondrous survivors from the dinosaur age, the seagoing turtles, and by dolphins and sharks. Many a giant Leatherback turtle has been choked to death by a bit of floating plastic mistaken for a meal. And if a turtle or a dolphin survives a few meals of plastic it faces another danger since the indigestible plastic can build up in its stomach and make it so buoyant that it can no longer dive for more fish and it eventually dies of hunger.

Extreme capitalism mobilises a quantity of materials unprecedented in human history. And the sheer scale of this mobility trains those who experience it to treat everything as disposable. Perhaps this is why personnel departments have morphed in the last thirty years into departments of Human *Resources*. When human beings become disposable resources, what chance have metal, plastic or timber that have fulfilled their purpose? The market accustoms us to things turning rapidly from fashionable lifestyle necessity to junk, waste product and landfill. Much of what the market presents us with is made of plastic, and designed to fail. But the plastic itself lasts for hundreds of years. Think of all the things that are sold as disposable: bags, batteries, cups, crisp packets, newspapers, pens, plastic bottles, plates and cutlery, contact lenses, cameras, mobile phones, magazines, printer cartridges, CD cases, cosmetic and detergent containers. And then add those things that are disposed of after a few months or a couple of years: computers, printers, tyres, clothes, umbrellas, hair straighteners, video cassettes and recorders; the list is endless.

How does living in a disposable culture affect the Church? Well the 'don't count on me' philosophy is not a good one for building stable and supportive communities of the kind in which the fruits of the Spirit such as patience and love and faithfulness can be learned and shared. Equally, faithfulness to traditional belief, and trust in God as the one whose love is the source of our truest happiness, becomes harder to sustain.

It is not just that the culture discourages us from being faithful but that it trains us to be faithful to certain things, fidelity to which corrodes our Christian commitment. Perhaps the strongest form of faithfulness our culture inculcates in us is fidelity to ourselves. And here Shakespeare, as so often, was the first true modern when he put in the mouth of one of his characters the motto 'above all else, to thine own self be true'.[11] But such a motto means we are discouraged from taking seriously duties and obligations that our relationships with others place upon us.

---

11   Polonius to Laertes in *Hamlet*, I.iii.78.

Equally our culture may enjoin us to be loyal to a brand, corporation or employer even when we find evidence of wrongdoing or the pursuit of unworthy ends. The whistle blower is regarded with considerable unease by organisations these days as the demands of managerial control and market survival are set above faithfulness to old-fashioned concepts of right and wrong.

Perhaps the most obvious abuse of such loyalty at the present time is the loyalty President Bush and Prime Minister Blair are demanding of citizens as they plan to attack a country already decimated by more then ten years of war, rationing and tyranny. When opponents point out the fickleness of their plans and intentions regarding Iraq – for example the fact that the British government secretly aided a British firm in the export of items to be used in the construction of a chemical weapons factory in Iraq in the 1980s – they are told that this is nonetheless a war in the name of morality, and a struggle of good against evil.

Telling the truth is a central part of learning to be faithful: so also is forgiveness. I am not suggesting that Saddam can just be forgiven, let off for his crimes. But what about the Iraqi people? Economic sanctions since the last Gulf War mean that food and medicines are rationed, and rationing has given far more power to Saddam than he would have had otherwise. This also made it harder for Iraqis to resist and develop democratic alternatives to this terrible man and his regime. And yet when one sees Iraqis interviewed on television it is obvious they are still among the most articulate and well educated of Muslim peoples.

Forgiveness is for Christians an absolutely fundamental part of fidelity. This is true in marriage and it is true in friendship. Without forgiveness we cannot be constant to one another because we are human and we let one another down. We put our own interests first, we are unfaithful, we are self-absorbed. Without forgiveness our relationships, the promises we make to each other would be shredded each time we lived as though we had not made them.

For the Christian true faithfulness involves acknowledging the potential of the other to become God's friend, to reflect God's image, to love God above all things. On the other hand sin obscures our companionship with God, mars God's image in us and misdirects our loves. But when we love God above all things, and when we recognise the transforming potential of this love in others, our other loyalties and loves are ordered aright. It was this potential which God acknowledged when God promised fidelity to the sons and daughters of men as we read in Genesis 9:6 – the only wickedness which will not be forgiven without sacrifice is the shedding of human blood 'for in their own image God made humankind'.

And as over time the sacrifices of bulls and sheep and doves failed to turn away the sin of the people of God, or to atone for their shedding of the blood of other people, God sent the Son of God to demonstrate God's ultimate faithfulness to God's people. Jesus Christ comes into a far country, under the power of an alien empire; he accepts baptism for sin though he never sinned even when tempted by Satan in the wilderness; he comes to preach the good news which is that when the people of God repent of their ways and turn back to God, that God will forgive them, will free them from the bonds of debt and sin, and heal their diseases. The cross is the terrible material form that God's faithfulness, God's constancy in love and friendship to humankind, ultimately takes. And this supreme act of self-sacrifice is presaged in the words 'You are my Son, the Beloved' (Luke 3:22), which is precisely the phrase the Greek translation of Genesis used of Isaac whom Abraham was about to sacrifice on the mountain when God provided the ram instead (Gen. 22:13).

God is so passionate about keeping faithful to God's people that God tears open the created boundary between earth and heaven in order to bring about God's will to restore them, to make them again the friends of God: the heavens are torn apart, just as the veil of the temple is ripped at the death of Jesus. God has come so near to us humans in Jesus and his sacrifice that every separating veil disappears between God and humans as well as between peoples.

The world tells us that human welfare can only be advanced by a constant process of tearing up promises, of ripping down old ways and loyalties, of abandoning traditional beliefs and spiritual practices. But the Bible from beginning to end tells a different story; that the faithful one, the righteous one, the happy one is like a tree planted by the waterside, drawing from its gradually spreading roots and branches the goodness of creation for its flourishing, growth and well-being.

Lent is a time when we seek to reorder our loves, to give up some cherished comforts, to open ourselves anew to God's passionate embrace. The Bible tells us that human promise-keeping, truth-telling, trust between strangers, and security between nations are only possible when we acknowledge our inconstancy, our unfaithfulness, our lies, and yet at the same time hold to the loving fidelity, the incredible constancy, the trans-forming truthfulness of our gracious God:

> *Gracious and upright is the Lord;*
> *Therefore he teaches sinners in his way.*
> *He guides the humble in doing right*
> *And teaches his way to the lowly.*
> *All the paths of the Lord are love and faithfulness*
> *To those who keep his covenant and his testimonies.*
> *For your name's sake, O Lord*
> *Forgive my sin, for it is great.*
>
> Psalm 26:8–10

6. Foot-and-mouth and the Market

March 2001

Go and tell that fox for me, 'Listen, I am casting out demons and performing cures today and tomorrow, and on the third day I finish my work.'

Luke 13:31–32

At the beginning of the outbreak of foot-and-mouth disease, which has virtually closed down the countryside of Britain and Ireland, the government and local authorities advised people living in rural areas not to go to church on Sundays for the duration of the outbreak. People mixing in church and travelling to church would likely spread the disease around and so the doors of many churches in rural Britain are locked this Sunday. At face value this might be seen as an act of self-denial on the part of rural people anxious for the welfare of their animals, and indeed town dwellers are making similar sacrifices by not going to the countryside for walks. But is more going on here than first meets the eye?

One hundred thousand animals have already been slaughtered on farms across England, Wales and Scotland and the government is talking of slaughtering up to half a million in total. The outbreak is without question an unmitigated disaster for a food and livestock industry still not fully recovered from the BSE crisis, and in addition suffering from drastic reductions in farm gate prices for meat and animal products, including milk, in recent years. But down at the local supermarket it is hard to get any sense of a crisis on the farms. Bulging supplies of fresh meat, milk, cheese, butter and yoghurt fill vast refrigerated aisles and delicatessen display cabinets.

Foot-and-mouth is a highly contagious virus that afflicts cloven-hoofed animals. It displays as blisters around the mouth and face, on teats and around hooves. Animals may experience lameness for the three- to four-week duration of the disease. Affected animals suffer some reduction in appetite and activity, just as humans do during a particularly heavy dose of influenza. Milk production also decreases for the duration of the disease. Mortality from the disease is low, though young animals are more at risk. Most farming communities around the world simply live with the disease and it is probably from one such – Argentina, Kenya or Thailand perhaps – that the disease first entered these shores in the latest outbreak, most likely in infected meat or meat-waste which was fed to pigs.

But if the disease represents no major threat to animal or human welfare, why is the whole countryside of Britain and Ireland, and of parts of the EU, closed down and on a virtual war-footing? Britain's agriculture policy still goes back to the food shortages which Britain experienced during the Second World War. After the war, the government decided that food production needed to be expanded so Britain could never again be at the mercy of hostile submarines threatening food supplies en route to our ports. And so for more than fifty years government policy has encouraged and subsidised farmers to uproot hedgerows and woodlands, and poison the fields, wildlife and waterways of Britain with a vast cocktail of chemical pesticides and fertilisers. It is this same policy that condemns millions of animals to life in cruel cages or confining stalls inside dark sheds, growing at unprecedented rates as they are fed on the remains of other animals or, post-BSE, on fishmeal dredged from the ocean in vast quantities. For most of their short lives before slaughter they are prevented from moving around in the open air where their growth will be slower.

It was forty years ago, not long after this policy was first conceived, that the Ministry of Agriculture, Fisheries and Food decided to go for a foot-and-mouth eradication policy. Australia was the first country to successfully eradicate the virus in the early twentieth century, followed by the United States and Canada. The decision was made primarily on economic grounds. Such are the cost margins arising from the quest for 'efficiency' in food production that delays in preparing animals for slaughter, or temporary reductions in milk yield arising from the virus, threaten profitability. It was in the early 1990s that Britain successfully lobbied her EU partners to adopt the same policy, although Poland and other non-EU countries, which practise less intensive and chemically dependent forms of farming, still have the disease.

And so the real reason for the closure of many churches in rural Britain during the outbreak is not animal welfare but profits. Christians are prevented from worshipping God together because the British state puts the freedom of large farmers and food corporations to make profits (albeit with the aid of government and EU subsidies) above the worship of God. And the enforced emptiness of the churches in rural Britain this Lent is indicative of a much larger emptiness in rural society today. The 'efficient' machines and sheds of intensive farming have replaced the communities of rural workers who sustained more extensive and kinder forms of farming in previous eras. Efficiency subsidies have destroyed thousands of small farms across Britain and it is only the very big producers who make serious profits from this subsidised efficiency. In consequence farming, especially on the near-extinct traditional small mixed farm, has become a very lonely and uneconomic occupation and suicide rates amongst farmers are at unprecedented levels. Not surprisingly we hear that the children of farmers no longer want to be farmers themselves and dozens of people get out of farming every week.

It is not only human communities that are affected. Bird and small mammal populations have drastically declined across rural Britain as the chemical cocktail of intensive farming has killed off the food chain of insects, on which wild birds and mammals depend. The 'silent spring' that Rachel Carson forecast more than forty years ago in her book of that title is now a tragic reality on the cereal prairies which have been bulldozed into existence across parts of our countryside. Rivers and groundwater are not exempt from the toll of farming efficiency. Slurry and waste from animal sheds are far and away the largest source of river pollution in Britain today, followed by nitrates from excess use of fertilisers.

The ancient Israelites had a very different attitude to farm animals than we do. They were nomadic herders and meat eaters and their animals were their principal source of wealth. Their culture involved an attitude of deep respect for animals, and their laws include many injunctions enjoining respect for animals and condemning animal cruelty. For the Israelites, as for most pre-modern peoples, the act of taking the life of an animal for human consumption was an event which required an expression of ritual respect when the animal was slaughtered. Hence all animals in Israel were supposed to be slaughtered only by Levites set aside for the task of serving the temple and offering sacrifice. And hence the violent shedding of blood was ritually cleansed of its moral endangerment. The burden of keeping to this practice was such as to significantly restrict the amount of meat eaten by faithful Israelite pastoralists.

By contrast modern intensive husbandry and slaughter methods show little respect to either animals or their maker. They reduce animals to commodities in a supply chain designed principally around the profit motive. Animals are carted up and down the country before slaughter to holding stations such as the one in Heddon-on-the-Wall, Northumberland, where the present outbreak of foot-and-mouth likely began. Such holding stations are not really farms at all: they are pre-slaughter factories where animals are fattened for two weeks before being shipped down the motorways again to the small number of large abattoirs that British supermarkets favour with their business. Evidence of inhumane treatment of animals at Heddon-on-the-Wall had been reported both to the local council and local animal charities. But when, three months before the foot-and-mouth outbreak, officials from MAFF visited the farm and found dead carcasses rotting in sheds housing live animals, they simply advised the farmer to clean up his act, and no further action was taken. Animal cruelty, even bad hygiene, was not to get in the way of profitable large-scale food production.

A few weeks ago I was sitting in a farmer's kitchen and picked up a book of cartoons issued by the National Farmers' Union to raise funds for farmers in need of assistance. One cartoon struck me in particular. It depicted the traditional annual display of Soviet military muscle in Red Square. And in the midst of the procession of rockets, tanks and soldiers was a man in a bowler hat and pin-striped suit standing up in the open top of a Jeep-style vehicle. Premier Breschnev is shown looking quizzical and he turns to the general next to him, points to the man and asks who he is. The general replies 'he is an agricultural economist: you should see how much damage he can do'.

The industrialisation of farming, the imposition of so-called free market economics on the growing and purveying of food, shows disrespect for animals, for land, for rivers and for the people who live and work on farms and whose lives are increasingly blighted by the farming crisis. At the root is an attitude to the animals and the land that displays deep disrespect for creation and its Creator. The coerced denial of worship in rural churches during the current crisis symbolises this lack of respect, and the mistaken priorities of an industrial food system that reduces the bounty of divine provision for human life to a system of globally traded commodities.

Gathering together to worship God is a subversive business in foot-and-mouth Britain. As Christians we meet together for worship because we believe that God has called us to break bread and to hear the story of God's way with God's world in local worshipping communities. At the heart of the story, and of the Eucharist in which we celebrate it, is the belief that the earth is the Lord's and that in Christ God has visited and redeemed his creation in the embodied form of our incarnate Lord.

Fragile bodies matter to God and we know this because God became a body to redeem life in the body. And communities, local communities, matter also. St Paul calls such worshipping communities the body of Christ. They symbolise and represent the calling of the whole creation to praise God and to live in peace.

The deregulated market economy which has given us BSE, and now the foot-and-mouth calamity, is a system which is at war with God's creation, and not at peace. It wrests produce from nature as though she will not give up her bounty unless subjected to technological torture and confinement. This war is not only against the welfare of the animals and the health of the soil, but also the very souls of farmers and of farming communities. Capitalism is a hungry god and visits cruelty and inhumanity on animals and people alike. The hidden costs of treating animals as globally traded commodities include the cruelty of their caged existence, and of long-distance live transportation, increased energy consumption and pollution arising from billions of 'food miles' between farm and plate, and the destruction of rural communities and the rural economy as small farmers and local abattoirs go out of business. None of these costs are picked up by the supermarkets who have fostered this system and who retail 80 per cent of foodstuffs in Britain, which maintaints the most centralised food economy in the world. And it is this system that delivered the foot-and-mouth virus so effectively and systematically across the whole country in just a few weeks from its first appearance in Northumberland.

Idolatry, the worship of that which is not God, is proscribed in the Bible because there is nothing, and no goal, in the created order which can be put in the place of God without doing dishonour to the Creator, and without threatening the welfare of the creature. Capitalism is a poor idol indeed and as Christians we are called to resist its idolatrous claims on our lives and our communities. The clearest way we can do this as I say is to sustain lively worshipping communities in which Christian habits and values are shared and sustained.

One of these habits is patience. The friends of Jesus became impatient on his behalf towards the end of his ministry because they saw his steady move towards Jerusalem as possibly resulting in disaster: 'Get away from here because Herod wants to kill you' they warned him. But Jesus replied as someone who had time and could be patient about it: 'Go and tell that fox for me, "Listen, I am casting out demons and performing cures today and tomorrow, and on the third day I finish my work" ' (Luke 13:31–32). Jesus knew what awaited him in Jerusalem and yet he did not resist this end but rather embraced patiently the suffering of the cross as God's way of reversing the impatience of the principalities and powers, and of their ultimate ally, death.

For Christians resources for patience arise from an observation of Jesus' preparedness to suffer death on the cross, and also, as Stanley Hauerwas puts it, from 'the narrative of God's patient care of the world' which the cross supremely displays.[12] Growing good food, nurturing children, creating community, all require patience and this patience carries its own reward. But the capitalist quest for efficiency and speed is the enemy of the virtue of patience. Some farmers are rediscovering the advantages of patience, of local food marketing, and organic production methods, and the respect for land and community that these habits show. Just as I was writing this a local farmer had a leaflet put through my door advertising 'Kitchen Garden'. They sell 'locally produced high quality, hand-reared and organic produce direct from the farm' and deliver it directly to my neighbourhood. I intend to give it a try.

---

12 Stanley Hauerwas with Charles Pinches, 'How Christians Should Be Sick', in *The Hauerwas Reader*, ed. John Berkman and Michael Cartwright (Durham, NC: Duke University Press, 2001), 365.

Passiontide

7. The Cross and the Cluster Bomb

March 2003

And the disciples went, and did as Jesus commanded them, and brought the ass, and the colt, and put on them their clothes, and they set him thereon.

Matthew 21:6–7

As Sky News and BBC News 24 displayed pictures from 'embedded' journalists of British and American tanks and armoured personnel characters rolling through the palm-fringed streets of Baghdad and Basra, the true extent of the carnage of Iraqi civilians that preceded these premature 'victory' processions has been hidden from public view in Britain and America.

A few days before the triumphal removal of the statue of Saddam Hussein from its plinth in the centre of Baghdad, American planes dropped cluster bombs in the region of the large town of Hilla, 80 kilometeres south of Baghdad, killing 61 and inflicting horrendous injuries on 460. Most of the injured were children. The tally of dead and injured is from the International Committee of the Red Cross (ICRC) in Iraq, whose spokesman Roland Huguenin-Benjamin reported seeing 'several dozens of bodies which were completely blown to pieces' in Hilla and 'dozens of severed bodies and scattered limbs'. All victims were 'farmers, women and children'.

Unlike British and American television, Al Jazeera has shown pictures from Arab cameramen employed by Reuters and Associated Press of babies cut to pieces in Hilla, of children's faces covered with embedded shrapnel, and of two trucks filled with the bodies of women and children outside the local hospital. Dr Hussein Ghazay at the hospital said that 'all the injuries were either from cluster bombing or from bomblets that exploded afterwards when people stepped on them or children picked them up by mistake'. After visiting the hospital Robert Fisk of the *Independent* wrote 'the wounds are vicious and deep, a rash of scarlet spots on the back and thighs or face, the shards of shrapnel from the cluster bombs buried an inch or more in the flesh. The wards of the Hilla teaching hospital are proof that something illegal – something quite outside the Geneva Conventions – occurred in the villages around the city once known as Babylon.'[13]

An Agence France Presse photographer reported seeing the tell-tale small parachutes which are attached to each tiny cluster bomblet in the streets of Hilla. The type of bomb deployed there, and throughout Iraq, is known as BLU-97 A/B. Canisters the size of a Coke can are delivered by high flying B-52s, or by American and British tanks and fixed artillery. The cluster bomb is technologically highly sophisticated and is designed so that around 50 metres above the ground it breaks open. Hundreds of tiny yellow bomblets are released and float down on parachutes exploding as they fall so that shrapnel is spread over an area equivalent to two football fields. The power of these multiple explosions can destroy a tank or it can rain death and injury on a hundred houses and their occupants if they are in the bomb drop zone. They spell instant death to anyone who is outside at the time. Residents of Hilla described how the bomblets seemed to fill the air with a 'voice of explosions' and the sky seemed to be 'raining fire'. Around five per cent of the bomblets usually fail to explode on impact, and so they become devastating but minuscule anti-personnel mines. Hilla residents saw many such bomblets in and around their houses, turning whole streets into killing zones long after the bombers had gone.

In the fog of war the phrase 'weapons of mass destruction', the ostensible reason the British joined this illegal invasion, has receded into the background. The talk now is of 'Brits' and Americans 'liberating the Iraqis' from Saddam Hussein and his reign of terror. Terrible physical evidence of the wickedness of his regime has already been uncovered in Basra by British troops.

13   Robert Fisk, 'Hail of cluster bombs leaves a trail of death', *Independent*, 3 April 2003.

But the only weapons of mass destruction – that is anti-personnel weapons which inflict indiscriminate death and injury by technical means contrary to the Geneva Conventions – seen in Iraq so far have been the cluster bombs, and Depleted Uranium shells, of American and British forces. The use of such indiscriminate technology is indicative of the psychology of what Samuel Huntington has called the 'lonely superpower' of the United States, which is willing arbitrarily to impose its will on the rest of the world by all means available, regardless of international law or basic human morality. When American generals were asked why they made the forays into Baghdad which they did last week, even though they then retreated, they said 'we did it to show that we can'. Presumably they would explain their use of cluster bombs in the same way 'to show that we can'. The rain of fire falling on the people of Iraq is a terrible portent in the skies of the technological prowess and the arbitrary amoral fiat of this new American empire.

Jesus chose a donkey and not a chariot to make his way into Jerusalem for his own final confrontation with the forces of evil. Pilgrims from Judea marked his path not with swords but with palm branches as he rode towards the temple. The event which Christians celebrate on Palm Sunday, and the events of Holy Week which follow, remind us that God trounced the fallen powers of human history, and the prince of darkness, not by might nor by sword but by the non-violent faithfulness of the Son of God. Jesus at his trial and on the cross called the bluff of the reigning powers, not appeasing but resisting their claims to dominion through his ultimate sacrifice. And by his death and resurrection he trounced the powers of this world, and 'led captivity captive' (Eph. 4:8). For St Paul, who wrote so many of his letters from an imperial jail, the cross is 'the power of God' (Rom. 1:16) which delivers Gentile and Jew alike from the 'power of sin and death' (Rom. 3:9). Liberation from the fallen powers comes not through the Son of God reigning from the skies but by the humility of the crucified Lord who 'gave himself for our sins to set us free from the present evil age' (Gal. 1:4).

As Christians unite around the world in opposing this war they are discovering that the cross can be reclaimed from its misappropriation by the Emperor Constantine, by crusaders, and by modern-day Christian imperialists. When we process with our palm branches and crosses this Sunday, and sing Hosanna to the Son of David, when we go in the Spirit of Jesus along the Stations of the cross on Good Friday, we proclaim and remember that 'God's weakness is stronger than human strength' (1 Cor. 1:25). The 'folly of the cross' is God's way of liberation and it has stood the test of time, while the arbitrary power and indiscriminate martial violence of empires has risen, and fallen, into the dust.

Easter

8. Crosses, Crusaders and Peacemakers

April 2003

Thus it is written, that the Messiah is to suffer and to rise from the dead on the third day, and that repentance and forgiveness of sins is to be proclaimed in his name to all nations, beginning from Jerusalem.

Luke 24:38

In the last three weeks we have celebrated in the liturgies of Passiontide, Holy Week and Easter the events of Christ's entry into Jerusalem, his last supper with his disciples, his betrayal, trial, scourging, crucifixion, death, and now his resurrection. At the same time as we have been revisiting these paradigmatic events in which we find the promise of our redemption, and the redemption of the world from sin, the combined armed forces of the United States and Britain have violently subdued and occupied the country wherein, according to the biblical witness, the first Fall of humanity into sin took place, in the Garden of Eden. The garden is described in Genesis as being situated between the Tigris and Euphrates rivers in Iraq, in what was once the great kingdom of Ur, and the first city state of Mesopotamia and on whose archaeological remains American troops have parked their tanks and tents.

The subduing and occupation of Iraq, and the terrible tragedy of thousands of lives lost, of hospitals and schools looted and burned, of ancient cultural heritage destroyed, was initiated by the leader of the most powerful nation on earth, the United States of America – or 'the last empire' as Gore Vidal, a citizen of that country, calls it. And the current American president, like the Emperor Constantine in the third century of the Christian era, is a convert to Christianity. Gore Vidal said a few weeks ago that both Bush and Blair are Jesus-lovers, and that is the problem. Even if they were not confessing Christians, Muslims throughout the world would still see the sacking and occupation of Iraq by the armies of Blair and Bush as an enterprise of the Christian West against a Muslim country.

For this is not the first time Britain and America have invaded and subdued Muslim lands. Ever since the tenth and eleventh centuries, and in particular the enterprises of King Richard the 'Lionheart' who unilaterally – that is without the support of the French – led his crusaders to a battle with Saladin for Jerusalem, which ended in a violent subduing and occupation of that city, Muslims have perceived their relation to the Christian West through the lens of the crusade.

Whence does the language of the crusade come within the Christian tradition? I confess that as a child I attended for many years an organisation which called itself the Crusaders. It had a logo which clearly referred back to the enterprise of the first crusaders. As well as attending weekly Crusader classes where we certainly did sing 'Onward Christian Soldiers' on occasion, as well as do Bible Study and other such things, I also used to go on Crusader Camps in the summer. Our round bell tents in fields, and camp kitchens and fires, were even a little reminiscent of the camps of the crusaders of old as they amassed in the desert to fight with the Muslims.

The Crusaders are a Christian evangelical youth movement whose central tenet of faith, like most modern Protestant evangelical denominations and parachurch groups, is that the atoning death of Jesus Christ on the cross was a terrible punishment involving torture and violent death which Christ underwent in payment of the penalty which human sin required a righteous God to impose upon the human race. And we were taught as Crusaders that it was only because Christ had paid this penalty and satisfied the wrathful judgment of God the Father that we were saved. The cross of Christ was presented to us in this way as the first crusade, and as the only possible way in which God could have redeemed the human condition.

For most of Christian history the Church has not made the theology of the atonement an article of creedal faith. The Nicene Creed in particular does not identify any one of the events of Christ's birth to a virgin, his life, death, resurrection, Ascension and gift of the Spirit – rather it invites us to confess and celebrate them all as the way in which God showed Godself to be 'for us' by becoming one with us in human flesh, while also remaining 'one, of one substance, with the Father'. And yet when I went to university I found that the evangelical Christian Union (CU) which I attended required of me to sign a different creedal statement in which I had to affirm that the one atoning and sacrificial death of Jesus was the redeeming punishment for my sins and therefore the key to Christian salvation. I served on CU committees, played the guitar at Christian missions, I went out with CU women, but I never signed the card. I did not believe then, and do not now, that this was a truthful account of a Christian understanding of salvation.

But, you may say, why all the fuss? After all, does not the imagery of sacrificial victimhood, of punishment for sin, have foundations in the New Testament, and not just in the InterVarsity Fellowship creedal formula? Before I try to answer the latter point I want to attend more fully to the former.

Why does it matter? It matters because if the central and exclusive saving event of Christian belief is a violent death by torture and crucifixion which is done to satisfy the unchanging demands of a heavenly divine judge who can do no other than demand violent satisfaction and punishment for human sin, then this sends a pretty powerful signal to all who follow in this religion that violent punishment is God's way of dealing with criminals, sinners and tyrants. Yes, the punishment has already happened, and for those who are Christian, who acknowledge Christ as Lord, it may be said that there is no occasion for further punishment. But for those who are not Christian, for those who depart from the narrow way, punishment, judgment, violence, even death, may be said to be still divinely ordained.

Religion is at its heart mimetic, as anthropologists are fond of pointing out. It is about acting out, copying, repeating, through rituals like Palm Sunday, and the Eucharist, the events which the gods are said to have marked out as the means by which a people have become their people. If the central event of the Christian story of divine salvation is about violent death, then it would be unsurprising if over their history Christians had not begun to copy, to act out this violent death, in their relations with people of other faiths, or in their punishment of criminals and heretics. And it was precisely this mimesis of violence and punishment which marked the Christian era from at least the tenth century onwards.

However until at least the fourth century most Christians were pacifists. They gave an account of their faith which did not allow them the option of the use of violence. This meant that Christians did not seek service in Rome's armies, they did not approve of capital punishment, and they did not use violence or the sword in their relations with one another or even those not of the faith. They would rather be subjected to violence as martyrs than resort to violence themselves. But if this was the early Christian position, when and why did Christians abandon it? What went wrong?

Christian art, as well as theology, is a wonderful source of information about the character of Christian faith through the centuries and it is notable that for the first four centuries the cross is rarely found as an image in Christian places of worship or in Christian mosaics and paintings. Instead we find the Chi-Rho – the stylised form of the first two Greek letters of the name of Christ – as the most common symbol of Christian belief, along with the fish and one or two other images. However by the fifth century the cross is increasingly used as a defining Christian symbol but only after the turn of Christianity into an imperial cult. And even then the cross images typically displayed not a dying and tortured Jesus but a risen and conquering Christ who is on the cross but clearly in the resurrected form of Christ the King. Only in the ninth century do we find the first images of a dead and tortured Jesus on crosses in Christian art, one of the first being a well-known wooden crucifix in Cologne Cathedral. Now this is terribly significant and reflects one of the great

theological innovation of the Middle Ages which was exempli-
fied in Anselm of Canterbury's book *Cur Deus Homo*, or 'Why
Did God become Man'. Anselm argues that the death of Christ
was a forensic and legal transaction between God and God's Son
in which the Son was killed in order to satisfy the legal requirements of the heavenly Lord for a price of redemption to be paid.
The analogies, the cultural context, for Anselm's writing are
drawn from the new form of hierarchical feudalism and sei-
gneurage which had overtaken the formerly relatively non-
hierarchical Anglo-Saxons and Celts of these islands as a result of
the Norman conquest – the French again!

Anselm's theological innovation placed the satisfaction theory
of the atonement at the heart of the Western Christian understanding of salvation history. It was taken up in due course by the
Reformers, and in the Counter Reformation, and it continues
to shape Catholic and Protestant theology to this day. And it may
be no coincidence that it was precisely at this time that the
Church began to practise violence against heretics, invented the
notorious Inquisition to deal with Catalan heretics, and adopted
a standing papal army, remnants of which can still be seen in the
fortified citadel of the Vatican to this day.

Not surprisingly therefore, the Anselmian theory has come in
for a good deal of criticism in recent times, not least from
feminist and black theologians, precisely because of its contex-
tual links with Christian and European imperialism, with the
violence of medieval Christianity, and feudal and later colonial
societies, and thence with patriarchy and racism. The lonely male
judge of feudal theology has acted ever since Anselm's day as a
legitimator of wars of conquest, of patriarchy, and of violent
forms of punishment, including torture and execution.

Instead of this violent atonement theory, early Christian theologians such as Irenaeus and Athanasius, and St Paul himself, laid
a much greater stress on Christ triumphant, who through the
totality of incarnation, crucifixion and resurrection enacts the
divine victory over sin, evil and the devil. For the early Christians
it was the resurrection and not the crucifixion which was the
determinative, the truly saving event, for as St Paul says 'if Christ

be not raised' then we are, of all men, most to be pitied. It is Christ as victor over death, the Risen and Ascended Christ, who leads captivity captive as St Paul has it. And it is only in the light of the resurrection that the sacrifice of the life of Christ can be seen as a saving sacrifice. It is not that it was not a sacrifice but to argue that it was the sacrifice alone, essentially, apart from the larger divine plan, which is truly saving – which is the true forensic and legal requirement without which God could not have saved the human race – to argue this is to misconstrue, to get deeply wrong, the true wonder and glory of our Easter faith.

I think now you can begin to see where I am going with this, why it matters. America is the most Christian nation in the West – 40 per cent of Americans claim not just to be Christian but evangelical Christians. But it is also the most violent of all the democracies which have been birthed since the Enlightenment. And the violence is not just directed towards America's enemies. A former postgraduate student of mine told me that he returned to the USA after the terrible events of 11 September 2001 and found that all his friends in Seattle, many of whom were active Christians, now carried guns whenever they went on public transport, and kept them in their houses. America punishes by execution more than any other Western nation, and Texas more than any other state. And America since 1945 has bombed or invaded 49 countries. Violence – Jessie James style, Rambo style – is the American way; it is at the heart of America's story about itself. The problem for us as Christians is that violence is also at the heart of American evangelical Christianity. The Southern states, which do the most executing, are the most conservative and evangelical states. The very same states which teach the doctrine of creation alongside evolution in their public schools are those states which execute the largest number of criminals. If religion is mimesis, and evangelical conservative Christians are committed to a view of their salvation which is intrinsically violent – which sets the necessity of violent punishment in the heart of the being of God, which even sets God as Father violently against God as Son on the cross – then the violence of America is Christian violence.

Now in defence of evangelicals we should recall that they are by no means all committed to the violent course that the American judicial system, American gun ownership and American foreign policy involves. They include powerful and prophetic voices such as Jim Wallis of the Sojourners Community who have long witnessed to peace. We should also acknowledge that it was the birth of America in violence – the terrible genocide against native Americans, and then the Civil War – which set its course, and that the military-industrial complex, as much as historical or religious orientation, has fostered the cult of gun-toting violence in America.

But there clearly is a problem about Christianity, atonement and violence, that we do well to be aware of as Christians, and that we should seek to understand; Jesus charges the disciples in the resurrection appearance we have just read to witness to a Gospel of repentance and forgiveness of sins to all the nations. This is the Christian witness, this is what resurrection means – not war or violent punishment, but mercy and forgiveness. Spreading this message may bring Christians into conflict with the governing powers. But when such conflict arises the Christian response will be peaceable if Christians truly remain faithful to the victory over sin and evil which was won with the resurrection of Jesus Christ from death on the cross.

This victory involved the first Christians in a clear conflict with the violence and wealth of the Roman Empire. The gospels clearly and unambiguously depict Jesus as a non-violent teacher. He teaches non-violence and he acts it out in his person and in the way of the cross. Living out the way of non-violence in a violent imperial culture means that he is killed though he is innocent. And it is precisely as the innocent victim that Christ's death opposes the violence of those who oppose the reign of God: his death unmasks the powers of evil, and renders empty their claim that peace and order are founded on violence. The reign of God is not founded on violence because God is from eternity a non-violent God. Violence is a consequence of the Fall of humanity – it plays no part in God's way with God's world.

The option of non-violence for the Church is not then simply an option – it is a requirement if we believe that God truly reigns, is truly victorious, in the resurrection of Jesus Christ. As Stanley Hauerwas puts it, 'Those who believe in the Resurrection perceive the true nature of power in the universe. Resurrection means that appearances can be deceiving. Regardless of what appears to be the case from an earth-bound perspective' – such as the seeming triumph of tyranny and war in human history since the first century – 'the Resurrection demonstrates the power of God's rule over all evil'.[14]

This is our Easter faith – it commits us not to the necessity but to the ultimate and divine impossibility of violence as a means to redeeming the human condition. Those Christians who claim that only through war can peace be attained are committed to another view of the atonement, a view which has to dismiss the non-violent teaching of the Jesus of the gospels as a perfectionist ethic, only good for monks and sectarians, pacifists who care not for the fate of the innocent, who would not resist tyranny. But it would be completely wrong to understand the Jesus of the gospels as one who commends non-resistance to evil. It was precisely his resistance to evil which entailed his following the way of the cross, and it is precisely in Christ as risen victor that we see that evil IS overcome, overthrown, not by violence but by the reign of a non-violent God.

> *Thus it is written, that the Messiah is to suffer and to rise from the dead on the third day, and that repentance and forgiveness of sins is to be proclaimed in his name to all nations, beginning from Jerusalem.*
>
> Luke 24:38

---

14 Stanley Hauerwas, *The Peaceable Kingdom: A Primer in Christian Ethics* (London: SCM Press, 1984), 88.

9. Resurrection Fishing

April 2000

And he said unto them, Cast the net on the right side of the ship, and ye shall find.
They cast therefore, and now they were not able to draw it for the multitude of fishes.

John 21:6

Eric Benns was, for much of his life, a trawler skipper in the North Sea. He fished out of the port of Lowestoft in Suffolk, which is located at the most easterly point of England. And the life of a fisherman was traditionally an uncertain one, as our Gospel this morning reminds us.

Sometimes Eric would return from a trip with a laden boat, and the price he got for the fish in the hold would cover the costs of hiring and running the boat and leave plenty in the kitty to pay off the men and give them all a bonus besides. On such days he would return home with some fish for his family, money enough for his wife to provide for the family and keep a roof over their heads, and plenty left over for him to spend with his mates at the British Legion Club over the road.

Other times Eric would return from a trip with less than half a load or stay out longer so reducing the men's time at home and their bonus share of the catch.

Fisherfolk like Eric were used to the uncertainty of life on the sea. They learned to depend on the sea, but not to expect every time to haul a full catch. This kind of life involved a dependence on nature which we find hard to imagine with our regular monthly salaries. It also meant people learned to live for the day, something again many of us are not good at with our life insurance policies, career goals and pension plans. Eric was no planner. It was his wife who ensured that whatever the fortunes at sea there was a steady income and savings to purchase the family home.

It is perhaps this sense of dependence on forces which are beyond human control which explains why it is that religious belief is stronger amongst people who live by the sea, and from the sea, than amongst people who live inland, or in cities.

In the last forty years fishing has changed, and changed dramatically. And the reason goes back to an earlier phase in Eric's life when he served on minesweepers in the Navy in the Second World War. Minesweeping was a risky and uncertain business. But the odds in the struggle against German mines and U-Boats in the North Atlantic shifted significantly with the discovery of sonar. With the aid of that characteristic pinging sound which sonar equipment emits, minesweepers could detect submerged mines, and submarines as well.

After the war sonar was put to civilian use and today all but the smallest fishing boats are equipped with the technology. And so today no well-equipped boat need return half empty. Sonar guides the boat to where the shoals of fish are and the nets come up full every time. And now the fish have nowhere to hide from the large nets and capacious freezers of the subsidised fleets of deep-sea trawlers which run out of the UK, France, Spain, Norway, Iceland, Russia and Canada. From the fishing grounds off Newfoundland to the Dogger Bank in the North Sea, cod, haddock, dab and plaice have shrunk massively in numbers in the last twenty years, so much so that the Canadian government has had to mothball whole fishing fleets and ban fishing altogether around Newfoundland.

Here in Europe we are likewise in danger of fishing out the seas. Already stocks of fish are dangerously low, and the fish that are caught these days are far smaller than the fish Eric and his men would have caught thirty years or so ago. Adult cod take many years to grow to full size, which can be as long as three feet. Few of them get the opportunity any more.

Like bulldozers and chain saws, oil wells and the internal combustion engine, sonar is one of many technologies which has transformed the relationship between humans and nature in the last thirty years. The authors of one recent global survey of ocean ecosystems found that the health and biodiversity of freshwater ecosystems right around the world have declined by 50 per cent since 1970 and those of ocean ecosystems by 30 per cent. And another scientific study of the state of the oceans in 2006 judged that many of the world's oceans could be deserts – all but cleared of life – within thirty years at present rates of destruction.

The human consumption of fish has more than doubled since 1960. And this is not by any means simply because of human population expansion. The majority of fish caught by trawlers around Britain are thrown back dead because they are the wrong type or size, or because of quotas on certain species. Deep-sea drift nets, as used by Japanese and Spanish deep-freeze factory ships, can be up to three miles wide. They take out everything from the ocean to a depth of more than one hundred feet regardless of its utility. Even in the North Sea indiscriminate drift net fishing is still used to dredge up marine protein as a source of food oil for use in pet foods, on fish farms and in some processed human foods.

We have come a long way from the world the disciples inhabited when they went fishing on the Sea of Tiberias in the weeks following the death of their leader Jesus of Nazareth. With no sonar they had fished all night without success. Their boat would probably have been hung with oil lights to attract the fish but that night this old technology had not worked. At daybreak they see a figure standing on the shore of the lake as they are coming in to land. He calls out to them suggesting they try again on the opposite side of the boat. And at last they strike it lucky, their small net almost breaking under the strain of the load of fish which was so big they were unable to haul it in.

John, described as the disciple whom Jesus loved, declares that this is not luck but a miracle whose agent is their crucified master. And Simon Peter, not waiting to debate the point, throws on some clothes, jumps into the water and swims back to land to greet his Lord on the beach. Jesus meanwhile is already barbecuing some fish on a fire for breakfast.

The Greek word for fish – *Ichthus* – is an acronym constituted of the first letters of the Greek words Jesus Christ, Son of God, Saviour. And the fish becomes a symbol of Christian faith in the first centuries. The early Christians also seem to have preferred fish to meat as a dietary preference. Early Christian art depicts Christians eating bread and grapes, water, wine and fish at Eucharistic meals but never meat.

Some blame Christianity for the technological rape and destruction of the natural world. Thomas Hobbes, the seventeenth-century Christian philosopher, suggests Christians ought to feel that they live in a world that can be measured, weighed and mastered and that they ought to confront it with audacity. Similarly Francis Bacon identifies science with power suggesting we achieve knowledge of the world in order that we may o'ermaster it.

However medieval theologians, like the early Christians, and the ancient Hebrews, believed that there were limits to human power in the world and that nature often suffers when humans pridefully neglect those limits. As Isaiah puts it

> *The earth is mourning, withering,*
> *the heavens are pining away with the earth.*
> *The earth is defiled under its inhabitants feet,*
> *for they have transgressed the law, violated the precept,*
> *broken the everlasting covenant.*
> *So a curse consumes the earth*
> *and its inhabitants suffer their penalty,*
> *that is why the inhabitants of the earth are burnt up,*
> *and few men are left.*

Isaiah 24:4–5

The book of Job speaks of God delighting in the extraordinary diversity that God has set into the creation from the leviathan who swims in the deep to the ostrich which runs and flaps its wings without being able to fly. God loves these wondrous creatures for their own sake, and because they reflect the glory of God. Humans are set in the land not to use it up or destroy it but to tend and nurture it, to enjoy its fruits without destroying its fruitfulness for future generations or for other animals. And in so doing humans can learn from nature herself:

> But ask the beasts, and they will teach you; the birds of the air, and they will tell you; or the plants of the earth, and they will teach you; and the fish of the sea will declare to you. Who among all these does not know that the hand of the LORD has done this?

Job 12:7–8

Surrounded as we are by our artificial technical worlds we are not good any more at listening to the earth, even when the earth pines and mourns for the destruction our technologies are wreaking. Perhaps the clearest instance of this is the collective refusal of governments, corporations and consumers to acknowledge the now very real threat that the earth will literally burn up with the excess greenhouse gases our technological civilisation is dumping in the atmosphere. This excess consumption is now hitting the earth's limits to absorb it. A human economy which is without limits has created an ultimate ecological scarcity in the earth system which is the capacity of the system any longer to absorb waste. And this limit now threatens to exclude poor African farmers and Bangladeshi fisherfolk from the basic necessities of food and dry land and potable water without which they cannot live.

The meals that Jesus eats with his disciples by contrast inaugurate an economy of abundance. The feeding of the five thousand is the paradigmatic meal of bread and fish in which the hungry are fed. In the barbeque on the beach this meal is recalled but set in a new light – the Risen Lord has triumphed over the powers of empire and sin which oppressed the people of God, excluded them from the land, and deprived them of nature's abundance. The Risen Lord inaugurates a new era in which there is to be no more killing or bloody sacrifice; sins are forgiven, debts repaid and peace between God and creation is restored.

And this peace between God and creatures brings a new era of companionship in which Christians are called again – like Adam in the garden – to be guardians or companions of other creatures and not domineering masters.

Hence when St Anthony, Jerome and the desert fathers of the third and fourth centuries went into the wilderness, like their Master, to commune with God and seek holiness, the peace they find produced a new relationship with all God's creatures as well as with God: hence St Jerome is often depicted plucking a thorn out of the paw of a lion, while others of these ancient saints are said to have harvested honey from bee hives without being stung.

In the lives of the saints we see that the world imagined in the book of Revelation by John of Patmos is not just some future millennial state beyond this life but on the contrary it is a new reality which is already breaking in to human history here and now.

That the angels are joined by all the living creatures in giving honour and praise to the Lamb is the source of our hope that, despite the continuing ravages of human sin and greed on the earth and its creatures, there is a divine intention to redeem creation, and that our own actions as Christians in caring for God's creation by attending to what we eat and how it is grown, and by reducing our reliance on machines that pollute and technologies that destroy, are in harmony with the grain of God's creation:

> *Then I looked, and I heard the voice of many angels*
> *surrounding the throne and the living creatures and the elders;*
> *they numbered myriads of myriads and thousands of thousands,*
> *singing with full voice, 'Worthy is the Lamb that was*
> *slaughtered to receive power and wealth and wisdom and might*
> *and honour and glory and blessing!' Then I heard every*
> *creature in heaven and on earth and under the earth and in the*
> *sea, and all that is in them, singing, 'To the one seated on the*
> *throne and to the Lamb be blessing and honour and glory and*
> *might forever and ever!' And the four living creatures said,*
> *'Amen!' And the elders fell down and worshiped.*
> Revelation 5:11–14

10. The Hallowing of Time

April 2004

And on the seventh day God finished the work that he had done, and he rested on the seventh day from all the work that he had done. So God blessed the seventh day and hallowed it, because on it God rested from all the work that he had done in creation.

Genesis 2:2–3

He that has seen me has seen the Father. He that believes in me shall do the works that I do.

John 14:9, 12

Sunday, the Lord's Day, on which Christians spend time with God, recalls the time when, having created day and night, sun and moon, earth, sea, trees and plants, humans and other animals, God rested from the labours of creation and blessed that day of rest and called it holy (Gen. 2:3). The rest of God on the original Sabbath is the blessed crown of all the hosts of living beings which God created. Recognition of this day takes centre stage in the commandments which God gives to Israel because the people of God are themselves identified as a sign of the restoration of that original state of blessed communion between God and creation which was the destiny of creation, but which was marred by human sin and evil (Exod. 31:13). On the Sabbath the people of God are reminded that their calling as God's people is for the worship of God on this day. There is no other destiny or calling or ethical purpose within creation which is higher or more significant than this. Worship and rest, glory and praise and enjoyment of the presence of God are the ends for which life is created.

From the era of the apostles, Christians have celebrated the Eucharist on the day of the resurrection or what Christians have come to call the Lord's Day. The phrase the Lord's Day, first recorded in Revelation 1:10, likely derives from the Lord's Supper. It is possible that the earliest practice of the Lord's Supper was a continuation of the Sabbath observance of the Jewish Christians in Jerusalem, and that the Eucharist would have been practised late in the evening of the Sabbath as the Day of Resurrection approached. The practice soon developed of the celebration of the Eucharist on Sunday morning as we know from references in the book of Acts, thus ultimately supplanting the Jewish Sabbath with the Christian Sunday. Christians continue to practise the Sabbath for as the writer to the Hebrews affirms the 'Sabbath rest still remains for the people of God; for those who enter God's rest also cease from their labours as God did from his' (Heb. 4:9–10). But Christians observe the Sabbath on the eighth day, the Day of Resurrection. In so doing they recognise that the Sabbath has been transformed by the resurrection of Jesus Christ, and that God's call to worship and rest is no longer just for Israel but for all people and the whole creation. This transformed practice of Sabbath is a pivotal element in Christian ethics, and its recent demise in Western societies has considerable implications for their moral character.

While establishing worship as a central and shaping activity of human life, Eucharistic worship on the Lord's Day also recalls the fact that God rested after the work of creation. That we can rest from our labours is indicative of the fact that God originally ordered all things well, and that God has reordered them in Jesus Christ. The worship, and rest, of the Lord's Day remind us that the creation was perfected and abundant when it was originally blessed by the Creator, and that the recovery of the divine benison is not therefore achieved through human actions. The rest of the Lord's Day is a reminder that in Jesus Christ God has already established a new redeemed physicality, a new time and a new space, within the boundaries of historical existence. Human work in the production of artefacts or of food and clothing is not then so central to the redemption of human life as moderns imagine, and certainly not so central that productive work cannot cease for worship and rest on the Sabbath.

The Sabbath has implications not only for human life but for all creation. Land and animals, even money, are all subject to the practice of the Sabbath according to Torah. Working animals were to be given rest on the Sabbath, each field in ancient Israel was to lie fallow for one year in seven, and debts were to be redeemed after seven years. This is why the peaceable kingdom which is envisioned by Isaiah (Isaiah 11) and is brought near in the life, death and resurrection of Jesus, is a kingdom which involves the whole creation (Rom. 8:19–22) and includes all forms of life on earth in the restoration of shalom, from the violent carnivore to the innocent child.

Sabbath rest is not just a break in the work of God in creation but the goal of creation and of all life in creation. God's nature is revealed in the fact that the end of the work of creation is this divine rest, and that he commands that his creation shares this rest to commune with him on this day. The command to rest is particularly momentous in the context of the increasingly long hours and unremitting character of paid work as it is experienced in contemporary Britain and North America. Business executives, lawyers, accountants, security personnel, shop workers and call centre staff are all increasingly subjected to the non-stop character of the 'flexible' labour market which the corporately controlled global economy imposes. While professionals and business people complain that mobile phones and emails generate a flow of demands on their time which does not stop when they are away from the workplace, many lower-wage workers find they have to take two or three part-time jobs to generate sufficient income to provide for their families. The Sabbath has then significant economic implications, for rich and poor alike are commanded to enjoy their rest on this day. Money itself is also supposed to rest on this day, and this is one of the reasons why usury is condemned in Jewish and Christian moral traditions until the Middle Ages, for interest on debt is an unceasing burden which does not rest in its accumulation on the Sabbath.

The increasing subjection of contemporary human life to the excessive demands of a global production system is a major consequence of the demise of the practice of Sabbath in contemporary society. The now much attenuated practice of closing shops and factories on Sunday in Europe and North America used to remind the world that God's work is not without end, and nor should our work be either. Sabbath rest established limits to the human economy and human work on creation, and the demise of these limits has significant effects on the human experience of work, and of life as a whole. The framing of human work by the weekly enactment of Christ's redemption of the world in the Eucharist gives a spiritual framework to human work without which work is always in danger of becoming idolatrous, not an accompaniment to the work of the creator/redeemer, but a total obliterating substitute.

The Sabbath's framing of the human work-a-day week shows up bad work, work which dishonours the Creator by unjustly exploiting people or destroying created order, for what it is, an idolatrous sacrilege against the Creator, and not only against humanity or creation. In modern society many people's experience of work is as the cog in the wheel of a mass production or service system, and the Sabbath commandment critiques this denial of human individuality and human freedom. Similarly the restlessness of modern production systems is indicative of the unholy and excessive demands of the corporate economy on the good earth that God gifted to us for our enjoyment and provision.

The Sabbath provides a holy boundary to human work which points up the spiritual nature of good work, work which is carried out in ways which respect and enhance the humanity of the worker and the artistry of creation. Eucharistic worship on the first day of the week, the Lord's Day, sets all our subsequent actions in the context of the story of the God who not only creates an abundant creation but redeems it from death and from scarcity. As Kentucky farmer and essayist Wendell Berry puts it 'the significance – and ultimately the quality – of the work we do is determined by our understanding of the story in which we are taking part'.[15] If we accept that in Christ we are free to be the

---

15   Wendell Berry, *Sex, Economy, Freedom and Community* (New York: Pantheon Books, 1992), 109.

people God intended when God first created human persons, then our work, our re-creation and our play, all take on a spiritual quality, and no activity, whether the construction of a house, the education of a child, the making of a meal or the playing of a piece of music can be considered as dishonourable or unspiritual, unless it is done badly, in ways which do not give glory to God, the first worker in creation.

For the German theologian Karl Barth the Sabbath command was the most important of God's commands because all forms of human moral agency, including good work and fellowship with other persons, are only made possible through the gracious action of God in Jesus Christ to redeem creation which Christians recall and celebrate in worship on the Lord's Day. All the other moral commandments are refracted and explained through the third commandment, for the ethical tasks and prohibitions to which the other commandments point are only meaningful and doable in the light of the graciousness of God in Jesus Christ which we recall and contemplate on the Sabbath. The Sabbath command, Barth says, 'reminds man of God's plan for him, of the fact that He has already carried it out, and that in His revelation He will execute both His will with him and His work for and toward him'.[16]

It is wonderfully ironic that a command to rest should act as the fulcrum and organising centre of the Christian moral life. Most moderns see ethics as a mode of reasoning which enables them to make decisions regarding particular actions in terms of their intrinsic nature or their outcomes. Christians also often understand ethics as that part of their faith or form of theology that is specific to Christian action. However this is to misconstrue the deep visionary and mystical orientation which runs through Christian ethics from the farewell discourses of Jesus in the Gospel of John, through the Christ and Spirit mysticism of St Paul, to the contemplative vision of God which Thomas Aquinas along with the medieval mystics saw as the greatest good that humans can experience, as the end or telos of life itself, and

---

16   Karl Barth, *Church Dogmatics:The Doctrine of Creation*, trans. T. H. L. Parker et al., ed. G. W. Bromiley and T. F. Torrance, Vol. III.4 (Edinburgh: T & T Clark, 1961), 53.

the essence of the life of heaven. It is also to misconstrue the deeply eschatological character of Christian as opposed to say Aristotelian or Kantian ethics for Christians believe not only that they are able to be good only as a consequence of their relation to God established in the worship of God's people, but also that the good ends to which they aspire have already been realised within human history in the incarnation of Jesus Christ as the end towards which all creation is already directed after his resurrection and Ascension. This puts the time-ful acts of remembering and anticipation at the heart of Christian ethics.

The practice of the Sabbath is not only a reminder to Christians of God's rest on the seventh day of creation, not only a call to worship and communion with God and God's people on the Day of Resurrection, but also a recognition that in Jesus Christ God has redeemed time from sin and futility. God in Christ has redirected our time towards the end for which we were created, which is to see God, to worship God and to enjoy his presence. This is why the burden of Jesus' moral teaching in the gospels is about God and not about human conduct, for as Jesus declares in the Beatitudes, 'Blessed are the pure in heart, for they shall see God' (Matt. 5:6). Moral purity, the good life, doing the will of God, is made possible for the Christian through an orientation towards God in worship and prayer whose end is the vision of God, but whose effects include a capacity for love and service towards the neighbour which Christians cannot find in themselves alone. This essential connection between seeing God and doing the will of God is also made in the Johannine farewell discourses. In response to the request of Philip that Jesus show the disciples the Father before he departs from them, Jesus declares 'He that has seen me has seen the Father' and hence 'he that believes in me shall do the works that I do' (John 14:9, 12).

The farewell discourses in the Gospel of John are an extended meditation on the significance of Jesus' absence from the disciples after the resurrection and Ascension, with the emphasis on the troubling aspect of his departure: 'Let not your hearts be troubled ... I go to prepare a place for you. And if I go and prepare a place for you, I will come again, and receive you unto myself' (John 14:1a, 2, 3a). 'Ye have heard how I said unto you, I go away, and come again unto you. If ye loved me you would rejoice, because I said I go unto the Father' (John 14:28). Later on Jesus speaks almost as if he is already absent: 'And now I am no more in the world, but these are in the world, and I come to thee' (John 18:11a). And Jesus also recognises that his absence presents those who follow him with the core moral dilemma of the Christian life, for they are left in the world, and moreover a world in which they no longer fit for it hates them, while Jesus is out of it, and can only pray that God will keep his followers from evil in his absence (John 18:14–16).

The moral dilemma that the absence of the One who is their moral exemplar poses for Christians is already anticipated in the conclusion of the farewell discourses; whether to identify with the world now that Christ has done his work – the Christendom option – or whether to withdraw from the world – let us call this the monastic option. The answer according to the Gospel of John is elegant and concise: Christians are to go into the world but not to be of the world (John 18:16–18). But as the history of the Church attests Christians have found it hard to discern what these polarising prepositions mean in the face of particular historical circumstances.

Christians are marked out in the world as those who believe that the end of created time and their own end have already been revealed in Jesus Christ. All historicist claims, such as the inevitability of moral or technological progress, or deferrals of justice to the poor and hungry – 'jam tomorrow' – are subverted by Christian eschatology which provides the basis on which Christians critique the 'falsely structured reality' of the present order. This does not mean that the Church can abandon its witness to that order but rather that the Eucharistic worship of the Church acts as the foretaste of the promised renewal of creation, and the source of Christian moral life, and of Christian witness to the world in the time between the Ascension and the Second Coming in which we now live. As another theologian, Douglas Farrow, puts it:

> The church, believing in the renewal of creation, offers
> an oblation which commits it to a life of responsible
> engagement with the world for the sake of its
> transformation. Not that the church itself can or will
> accomplish this transformation from below, so to speak,
> or assist the world to do so. The renewal which it seeks
> is hid with Christ in God – there is no nascent
> liberation theology here, nor hint of triumphalism.[17]

The oblation of liturgical time, time and silence, music and celebration, set apart for God on the Lord's Day, presents the worshiping community with a weekly experience of redeemed time in which the hidden end of human time is already displayed in the perfection of Christ in whom death is overcome by life and all things are made new. Instead of human time being a meaningless progression from birth to death, and cosmic time being the birth and death of the sun, time is revealed as findings its origin and fulfilment in Christ who is the Alpha and the Omega, and in whose resurrection and Ascension Christians discern the meaning of the future. Because Christians already know their end, and the end of creation, this means they are released from fear of the dead or of the past, and from anxiety about the future.

It is this confident eschatological orientation towards an already revealed future which explains the ambiguous civilisational power of Christianity in history. Hopeful orientation towards the future is a source of great energy and dynamism both for the individual and for society, but it is ambiguous because this future orientation has become secularised since the Renaissance and the rise of modernity. Modern humans believe they are autonomous within time and hence the source of their own redemption and their own future. States and corporations put technologies into the service of the construction of this humanly redeemed future even at the cost of destroying present ecological wealth and beauty for present and future generations. But tech-

---

17 Douglas Farrow, 'Eucharist, eschatology and ethics', in David Fergusson and Marcel Scott (eds.), *The Future as God's Gift: Explorations in Christian Eschatology* (Edinburgh: T & T Clark, 2000), 72.

nologies cannot redeem us from the ecological apocalypse towards which those same technologies are inexorably driving the planet. Neither global warming nor species extinction are being significantly addressed by the deployment of more beneficent technologies at the present time. Christians who believe that the world is already revealed as a new creation can resist the temptation to believe that technology can save for we know that it is only by reorienting our lives towards their renewal in Christ that we can find fulfilment and meaning in time, and hope for eternity. Christians can also be confident that we can take time to do things more slowly, take time to recycle and reuse, time to walk instead of taking the car, time to grow food or visit the farmers' market, for God has given us time and we don't have to justify every minute in terms of monetised production.

And so it is that Sunday by Sunday we can meet and gather here to 'waste time' together in an economically unproductive activity – worshipping God and celebrating communion, with God and with one another. Our gathering here to praise and pray and participate in this mystic feast indicates that for us as Christians there can be no true work, no true economy, no true relation, in a world, a workplace or a week that is not framed by such worship, and by the hallowing of time that is the Lord's Day, the Christian Sabbath.

Ascension

11. The Best Things in Life are Free

October 2004

*For unto every one that hath shall be given, and he shall have abundance:
but from him that hath not shall be taken away even that which he hath.*

Matthew 25:29

I was walking in Edinburgh's Botanic Gardens, enjoying the rich
colours of the trees in all their autumnal glory set off as they were
by a wonderful crisp clear blue sky, when on a small hill studded
with chestnut, beech, maple and oak trees I met the family of a
colleague who is a professor of economics and whose children
had almost completely buried him in leaves. I found this an
engaging sight – not just because of the joy of my friends so
evidently enjoying each other out of doors, but also because of a
lecture I had heard him give which was devoted exclusively to
mathematical models of the supply and use of money. Resources
are only really interesting to economists when they have the
potential through monetary activity and market behaviour of
becoming scarce, for only such resources are capable of generating surplus value. Now leaves are a resource which in the autumn
are by no means scarce. And yet here was a professor of economics and his family deriving one of the most valuable experiences
that this life has to offer – the bonding and intimacy of parent and
child – through the mediation of a resource which so long as
there are trees is unlikely ever to be recognised as valuable to an
economist.

The Parable of the Talents in St Matthew's Gospel is sometimes
read as a kind of Christological warrant for the modern
economy, for example by Margaret Thatcher in a speech to the
General Assembly of the Church of Scotland in May 1988,
subsequently dubbed the 'Sermon on the Mound'. In the parable

the master gives his servants a substantial sum of money – a talent roughly equates to £1,000 in today's money – and when he returns from a far country he heaps praise on those servants who were able to show they had put their talents to good use by diligently trading with them, while he sends into outer darkness the one who lazily buries the talent in the ground and digs it up on his master's return.

But the fathers of the Church read the parable in an entirely different way. For Origen the Parable of the Talents is an allegory in which the nobleman is Christ who leaves his disciples at the Ascension, while those given the talents are the disciples, entrusted with the ministry of the Word which has been given to them until he comes again. For St Chrysostom, the principal lesson of the parable is that we are to be diligent in proclaiming the Word in service of Christ, and in admonishing and instructing others to follow him. And equally we are to avoid the spiritual slothfulness of the man who just sat down and buried the gift of God's Word in the ground. For, Chrysostom says, we all, like the widow who gave her mite, have talents, capacities, with which to contribute to the common good of all and it is by being diligent in the use of them that we may attain to heaven 'for nothing is so pleasing to God as to live for the common advantage'.

We live in diligent times. Most of us in the UK who are in employment work longer hours than our fellow Europeans. Work is taking over our lives. I was talking a few days ago to a fire station engineer who used to run a Boys' Brigade troop on his weekends, but new flexible patterns of working have been introduced which require him to work whenever the need arises and he can no longer set aside the regular weekend and evening sessions which he needed to be able to run the Boys' Brigade, and so contribute to the good of his community.

It is as if economic diligence is running riot and knows no bounds; everything, even time itself, is being eaten up, being made scarce, by the gargantuan leviathan of the modern economy. So diligent have the large trawlers which plough the North Sea been in recent years that scientists warn that cod and haddock are close to extinction in our oceans. So diligent have our farmers been in digging up hedgerows and spraying their fields with pesticides and herbicides that bird numbers are diminishing to the point where Rachel Carson's prediction of a silent spring is sadly coming true. You are more likely to hear a dawn chorus in a city garden than on one of the vast prairies of the diligent chemical farmer. But so diligent have our car producers been that there is often not enough space for all the cars on city streets, and people are applying to their local authorities for permission to concrete over their front gardens to give themselves a parking place.

Time is running out for many species on this small planet of ours and maybe for us as well. So diligent have chemists and industrialists been in synthesising new compounds that the very health of human sperm is threatened by the environmental ubiquity of so-called gender-bending chemicals, that is synthetic substances such as pesticides and plastic softeners or phalates, which mimic human hormones, and in particular the action of oestrogen, when ingested by the human body. And perhaps it will only be when humans begin to feel threatened by ecological catastrophe that they and their governments and corporations will be prepared to be less diligent in growing the economy and more diligent in caring for the earth.

A lot of people think that religion – and perhaps especially Christian beliefs about the kingdom of God and the end of the world – are actually the problem rather than the solution so far as the ecological crisis goes. But the truth is that the more we on this planet devote ourselves to the gargantuan economy of material consumption the more threatened the planet becomes. It is not the belief in paradise, or the life of the Spirit, but the materialist belief that this life is all there is and we had better get as much out of it as we can so long as it lasts, which is really doing in the planet.

And here we come close to the heart of the Parable of the Talents. For it is spiritual sloth against which the parable is directed. And it is spiritual sloth which is the disease from which we suffer in these times. Advertisers and marketers have us, or at any rate many of our contemporaries, in thrall to the latest technologies and gizmos, clothes designs and electronic entertainment devices. But the more we devote our energies to these things the more we are distracted both from diligence in following Christ, and diligence in caring for one another and for the living species with which we share God's glorious creation.

The tree that was cut to become the cross of Christ was just one of trillions of trees that have grown on this planet. But it was a tree which reminds us in its humble but cataclysmic and world-changing service that every act of devotion, of sacrifice, of service, is a small exchange for the astonishing abundance which the Creator first showed when he showered this earth with the myriad diversity of more than ten million species. That holy tree is a powerful symbol of the generosity of the Creator in restoring to its original end the fallen order of the material creation which since Adam had become subject to futility. In response to the generous gift of new life which is offered to us and to all creation in the resurrection of Jesus Christ the Parable of the Talents urges us to be generous in sharing the gifts that are in us.

Spiritual generosity toward God and our fellow beings is a massive contradiction to the economistic quest to create scarcity – it is the spiritual secret, the mystic key which contradicts the law of sin and death and decay which is all around us as we continue to bury the discarded talents, the good gifts of God's glorious universe in landfill sites, and as more and more billionaires horde the surplus of the great economy of the earth while millions of other people lack the most basic necessities for a dignified life.

It was spiritual generosity which drove and sustained that great ecological saint, Francis of Assisi, to abandon the riches of his father's house and dwell in a poverty so radical that it shook the luxuriant living of cardinals in Rome. In modern times there have been few more effective in proclaiming spiritual generosity as the principle on which all life is built, and by which all life is intertwined in the wondrous resurrected life of Christ, than Gerard Manley Hopkins, whose poem 'As Kingfishers catch fire'

drips with the joyous recognition of the free grace that is offered
up to each one of us who opens her eyes and trains them on the
wondrous world of creatures:

> As kingfishers catch fire, dragonflies draw flame;
> As tumbled over rim in roundy wells
> Stones ring; like each tucked string tells, each hung bell's
> Bow swung finds tongue to fling out broad its name;
> Each mortal thing does one thing and the same:
> Deals out that being indoors each one dwells;
> Selves — goes itself; myself it speaks and spells,
> Crying 'What I do is me: for that I came.
> I say more: the just man justices;
> Keeps grace: that keeps all his goings graces;
> Acts in God's eye what in God's eye he is —
> Christ. For Christ plays in ten thousand places
> Lovely in limbs, and lovely in eyes not his
> To the Father through the features of men's faces.

12. Absence and Ambiguity

May 2003

And now I am no longer in the world, but they are in the world, and I am coming to you. Holy Father, protect them in your name that you have given to me, so that they may be one, as we are one.

John 17:11

Ever since the appointment of Rowan Williams as the Archbishop of Canterbury, 'Reform'-minded evangelicals have been suggesting that his appointment is against the will of God, that he is too liberal to be a public guardian of the faith, and that he is opposed to the unity and truthfulness of the Church, all because of his views on sexuality. Many are proposing to stay away from the 2003 National Evangelical Congress in protest at the invitation to Rowan Williams to be present and offer a prayer at the meeting, although he has not even been invited to address the congress. The issue which sets the evangelical Reform group against Rowan Williams concerns the place of homosexuals in the Church and in particular in the ministry. Bishops and archbishops who have knowingly ordained priests who are in long-term, stable and faithful homosexual relationships are said to be heretics because they are in disagreement with the official Anglican position, as affirmed – albeit with considerable dissent – at the 1998 Lambeth Conference that such ordinations, and such relationships, are wrong and against the historic traditions of the Church.

In reported comments in *The Times* last week the private view of Rowan Williams is said to remain 'that an adjustment of teaching on sexuality would not be different from the kind of flexibility now being shown to divorcees who wish to remarry, or the softening in the 16th century of the Church's once total opposition to borrowing with interest or the 19th and 20th century shifts of view on subjects like slavery and eternal hellfire.' But alongside this statement of his privately held view, the Archbishop has also formally declared his intention to uphold the official position of the Church at Lambeth in 1998 that same-sex unions are opposed to biblical teaching and that the Church cannot publicly approve such unions either by ordaining those in such unions, or by the use of public rites of blessing on them.

Some will accuse the Archbishop not only of heresy at this point but also of hypocrisy – how can he think one thing privately and uphold another position in his official statements and practices?

In today's Ascension-tide gospel we find Jesus in contemplative mode reflecting on the implications of his coming bodily absence from the disciples for their future as public witnesses to the divine truth of his Sonship and redemption of the world. His prayer for the disciples, repeated a number of times, is 'that they may be one, even as we are one'. And the basis of that unity is the mystical relationship between the disciples and God which is analogous to the relations of the Father to the Son: 'as you Father are in me and I am in you may they also be in us' (John 17:21) and again 'the glory that you have given me I have given them, so that they may be one, as we are one, I in them and you in me, that they become completely one, so that the world may know that you have sent me and have loved them even as you have loved me' (John 17:22–23).

The means of the oneness of the body of Christians is the same means by which the Son is one with the Father and this according to the Gospel of John is the relationship between Jesus and the Spirit whom John the Baptist saw 'descending from heaven like a dove' and remaining on Jesus. And John the Evangelist leaves us in no doubt that it is this same Spirit who is given in turn by Jesus to the disciples after the resurrection of Jesus before the Ascension, and hence before the Day of Pentecost. John has it that in the second resurrection appearance of Jesus – he had earlier appeared to the women in the garden but not to Peter or the others who came to be called apostles – after saying 'peace be with you' and 'as the Father sent me so I send you' he then 'breathed on them and said to them "Receive the Holy Spirit. If you forgive the sins of any they are forgiven and if you retain the sins of any they are retained" ' (John 20:21–22). So if we ask how were the disciples to know what to believe and how to live after Jesus had been taken from them, the answer according to John is quite plain – it is through their relationship with God the Spirit. Just as the 'Spirit of truth' gave authority to the words and works of Jesus so the same Spirit will 'lead the disciples into all truth'.

Now this is all a bit confusing, for the tradition which we celebrate in these days of waiting between the Ascension and the day of Pentecost is that Jesus ascended to heaven to be seated on the right hand of God and only some days later did the disciples receive the gift of the Holy Spirit in the upper room in Jerusalem. Who is right? The Gospel of John who puts the gift of the Spirit into the midst of the resurrection appearances, or the writer of Luke-Acts who puts it after the Ascension of the Risen Lord on the day of Pentecost?

What we are faced with here is ambiguity, and accounts of events which varied between the different churches to which John and Luke – the gospel writers – themselves belonged and in which the stories of Jesus and the first disciples had likely circulated for some years in oral and possibly textual form before being consigned to the authoritative written texts of the gospels. And this is not the only aspect of the life and ministry of our Lord on which the gospel writers disagree. John has the scourging of the temple at the beginning of Jesus' ministry while the other evangelists put it at the end. Even the Synoptic writers disagree on significant details such as the content of the famous Sermon on the Mount, and the wording of Jesus' reinterpretation of the Jewish law, or the events around the passion, death and resurrection of Jesus. These disagreements have led modern scholars to argue that John is not as 'historically accurate' as the other evangelists, and to argue that there may even be a more authoritative and ancient gospel account – sometimes called 'Q'

– behind the Synoptic Gospels, if only we could find it (and some have suggested it is underneath the altar at Rosslyn Chapel!).

Our forebears though do not seem to have been troubled as some modern scholars are about the differences in emphasis and narrative between the different gospels. Similarly there seems in the early Church, and right through to the Middle Ages, to have been a greater latitude of belief and practice on a whole range of issues – including sex before marriage and same-sex unions – than the churches of the post-Reformation, or what we now call the modern era, have tended to allow.

Modernity is simply a word for newness but it has come to be taken to represent that period of the rise of natural science and of the domination of reason – rather than religion – in human affairs which took its rise from the Renaissance and reached its finest flowering in the Scottish, French and German Enlightenments. One of the most prominent features of the modern cult of reason was a quest for certainty and unanimity in human affairs from ethics and the law to medicine and physics which was never sought by the medieval philosophers or theologians. Whereas theologians in the Middle Ages had relied on case law as a means of discerning the moral and legal rectitude in particular situations, by the eighteenth century casuistry had fallen into disrepute and first the Pope, and then in the nineteenth-century fundamentalist theologians, sought to claim inerrancy for their particular formulations of the Word of God, as though particular written formulae were universally transparent to all people everywhere whatever their particular cultural circumstances. One famous example of this tendency was the imposition of monogamy on many colonised peoples by nineteenth-century missionaries who had little sensitivity to local custom and as a consequence turned many women out of their own homes and forced them into prostitution.

Where did this quest for certainty come from? According to the philosopher Stephen Toulmin it seems to have originated in the wars of religion of the sixteenth century, which issued out of the struggles between Protestants and Catholics, merchants and prelates, right across Europe and produced a political situation in which kings were assassinated and individuals or whole churches declared heretical, or even burnt at the stake, for holding to one or other doctrinal and liturgical confession.[18] The most common cause of disagreement concerned the precise manner in which Christ could be said to be present in the bread and wine of the Eucharist. Catholics and Protestants alike sought to lay down the law on exactly how Christ's words 'this is my body broken for you' were to be understood.

The struggles over doctrine and liturgy of the sixteenth century led many in seventeenth- and eighteenth-century Europe to seek to reduce the influence of religion over human affairs. But they led at the same time to a new quest for certainty, a desire for unambiguous foundations for truth, both in natural science and in moral and political and social matters, which earlier generations had never desired or expected to attain. The outcome was the sovereignty of reason and the birth of nation states said to be governed by universal values, such as those of liberty, equality and fraternity announced, albeit with great violence and bloodshed, in the French revolution. The newly published constitution of the European Union similarly excludes any reference to a spiritual or divine foundation for the values which the Union and its member states seek to uphold.

We live in what some call a postmodern age, in which the sovereignty of reason seems to be in doubt. Fewer of us now believe that science and reason can automatically deliver the gradual improvements in human welfare and happiness than those of previous generations. And yet the quest for certainty remains. David Blunkett as Home Secretary – to give one recent example – has announced his intention to impose a tariff of a life sentence, and even of a particular length of years by which life is to be understood, upon a sentence of murder. But the English legal tradition has retained, against this laying down of a precise number of years for a particular crime, a premodern respect for casuistry and context and character which the modern quest for

---

18 See further Stephen Toulmin, *Cosmopolis: The Hidden Agenda of Modernity* (Chicago, University of Chicago Press, 1990).

certainty has largely erased from public and political life. And so the Home Secretary stands in opposition not just to the chairman of the Bar Council but to a whole historical tradition of interpretation of human rights and wrongs on a case-by-case basis. And this reflects a larger problem with ambiguity in modern British political life – it is as if everyone has to sing from the same hymn sheet the whole time and there can be no room for disagreement and rational debate within a cabinet or a government or even a political party without undermining its putative authority, strength or power. And so we have strong-arm political leaders in both Washington and London who impose by email and even SMS messages their own particular views on those around them with absolute certainty. They require their ministers and democratic representatives to adopt them with equal certainty even when these views rest upon highly ambiguous evidence: the case of the non-existence of weapons of mass destruction in Iraq is just one particularly prominent recent example of this tendency.

The quest for certainty, whether in sexual morality, ecclesiastical or civil law, or political judgment, remains a feature of our age. But it is becoming clearer and clearer that this quest is at odds with the ways in which people, and Christians, through the ages, have in fact managed to live with ambiguity and diversity and disagreement without resorting to heresy trials, threats of schism or war. Far from appealing to one line of dogmatic pronouncement, or one universally received theory, in the past clerics and philosophers discussed particular moral cases in the light of a range of traditions and in the light of particular contexts and cultural circumstances. The unity of Christendom was maintained from Scotland to Sicily and from Poland to Portugal not by an inerrant and domineering papal authority imposed willy-nilly on every circumstance but by argument and discussion in particular locales and around individual cases. And it was the increasing speed of communication, and the consequent tendency of the papacy to impose its increasingly corrupt practices and views on Christendom from one end to the other, which eventually led to the Reformation and the break-up of the one united Europe, which we are now in the process of trying to reinvent again in secular guise.

What I am saying then is that for a very long time the prayer of Jesus for his disciples – that they might be one even as he was one with the Father – did indeed find an answer but it was not the kind of oneness that the modern sovereignty of reason, and the quest for certitude, have led us to expect. The point was not that Christians in different places and from different cultures did not do things differently – there is plenty of evidence of such differences, as say between Jewish and Gentile Christians even in the New Testament. The point was that they 'agreed to differ' in the time-honoured phrase. They remained in relationship, they belonged to one body, one social organisation, even when they differed over certain matters of belief and practice.

And this means that Christian truth does not give access to moral or doctrinal theory which is on every point unarguable and universally applicable. The point rather is that how we know the truth, and how the truth sets us free is through the Spirit, through our relation to God and through the relations of love which God the Spirit makes it possible for us to enjoy with one another. Love and knowledge for St Paul and St John, as for St Augustine, are intimately related. It is not possible to know the truth, let alone to do the truth, unless we are already loved by the Father and indwelt by the Spirit. As the epistle of John puts it 'those who believe in the testimony of the Son of God have the testimony in their hearts' (John 5:10). Truth and emotion, theoretical knowledge and practical experience, are not in separate compartments for John. They belong together. And this is precisely the meaning of the spiritual character of truth for John – it is only through loving God that we have true knowledge of God. There is no propositional formula, papal encyclical or statement of evangelical fundamentals which can guarantee that we are lovers of God, or that God loves us. We can only know this in the particulars of our bodies, emotions, experiences, relationships, and thoughts. But this does not mean that we are alone with the truth. On the contrary if truth is only knowable through relationships then it is in relationship with one another that we come to be able to reason our way toward truthful living and truthful believing.

The idea that Rowan Williams has to agree with every jot and tittle of the Church's official position on sexuality, both publicly and privately, or else he cannot be a true archbishop, cannot be a site of unity for the Anglican Communion, is itself not a truly conservative notion but quite the opposite; it is a highly modern one. It is redolent of the quest for certainty, of the sovereignty of reason, and the desire for knowledge without spiritual relations, without love, a desire which in the context of the wars of religion of the sixteenth century may be quite understandable, but which nonetheless is not in accord with traditional Christian and scriptural accounts of how we know and live the truth of God. If there is no discernment required in particular cases, if we dare not argue for fear of falling out, then why do we need the Spirit to lead us into the truth, and to make us one? We just need to write down a list of instructions about morality and doctrine and sign on the dotted line. This is not the protection for which Jesus prays for his disciples. But it is strangely reminiscent of the kind of thought control that modern totalitarian states have tried to exercise over their citizens. And there is plenty of evidence that the neo-conservatives of the United States are pushing academics and clerics and citizens in general in the same direction – books are being banned from public libraries, academics and journalists silenced, and real argument, real dissent not tolerated.

This is not the unity we seek as Christians – it is on the contrary precisely this kind of thought control which has been the source of war and conflict, and yes of religious war, through Christian history. Let us pray God that Jesus' prayer for his disciples is once again owned by Christians today in the Anglican Communion, among evangelicals both here and in the United States and throughout the Christian Church – and the promise of this prayer was not demeaning conformity or suppression of liberty and dissent but rather 'that they might have joy made complete in themselves' (John 17:13).

Pentecost

13. Pentecostal Politics

October 2000

The members of the body that seem to be weaker are indispensable, and those members of the body that we think less honourable we clothe with greater honour, and our less respectable members are treated with greater respect; whereas our more respectable members do not need this. But God has so arranged the body, giving the greater honour to the inferior member, that there may be no dissension within the body, but the members may have the same care for one another. If one member suffers, all suffer together with it; if one member is honoured, all rejoice together with it.

1 Corinthians 12:22–26

At a conference of business people in London in September, Tony Blair declared once again that New Labour is the party of business, and that the party's task in government will be to prepare the United Kingdom for more effective competition in the new global marketplace. Globalisation is without doubt a central feature of our times and it is surely right that New Labour should seek to hone its vision of a better Britain to the new shape of global economics, and global politics. However as well as seeking to respond positively to globalisation it is also important to develop a critical response to the global forces which are now upon us, and the new politics and economics they tend to favour.

One of the most troubling features of globalisation is the insecurity of employment which a growing proportion of the populace of Europe experience in the newly mobile world of globalised capitalism, and the related growth in income inequality both regionally and globally which the deregulated world of global capitalism brings in its wake. Another unfortunate feature of globalisation is the homogenisation of culture which the greater mobility of artefacts such as television programmes, computers or fast food brings in its wake. And these two aspects of globalisation are not unrelated, for the ethical and spiritual values which have sustained the socialist and Labour movements in the quest for security of employment and reductions in inequality between rich and poor are closely related to the roots of socialist political culture in the particular history and traditions of Europe, and especially the Jewish and Christian traditions.

The current remaking of the image and identity of the Labour movement in Britain risks obscuring the cultural origins of the struggle for egalitarianism, liberty and social democracy from which the Labour movement was born. Another risk, as the party seeks to reshape its policy and membership 'machine' to a more mobile, electronic and globalised society, is that the centrifugal tendencies of such a move will suppress the traditional roots of the party in local community-based politics, which made the Labour party less amenable to the modern 'on-message' machine politics but more genuinely participative.

Over the summer I read biographies of two people who were deeply formative of the traditions of democratic socialism. The first is John Keane's magnificent biography of Tom Paine, and the second Fiona McCarthy's compendious biography of William Morris: two very different people from two very different centuries. One of the things that united them was a fundamental trust in the gifts and abilities of ordinary people, and the belief that the essential goal of a just as well as effective political culture is the mobilisation of the inherent creativity of all the members as citizens of a genuine political community. Paine's great influence in the American and French revolutions was in sharp contrast to his treatment in Britain as a dangerous subversive and, as Will Hutton points out, it remains one of the defining features of modern Britain, as contrasted with either France or the United States, that because of the failure of the English revolution we have never established a political culture in which the people of the country are truly citizens and not just subjects. Morris was much more a man of the establishment, educating the aesthetics and shaping the interiors of many of the English middle and upper classes with his famous designs and workshops. But Morris also believed in the inherent creativity of working people, and in their capacity, their right, to self-sufficiency and a decent living, through the exercise of their own craft skills, and through democratic management of the machines and processes of manufacture.

While neither Paine nor Morris were confessing Christians – indeed Paine became vociferously anti-religious in later life – nonetheless the biblical origins of the ideals of self-government and self-sufficiency, rooted in a belief in the inherent God-given creativity of ordinary people, are clear. The traditional Jewish and Christian vision of economic livelihood as self-sufficiency, encountered for example in Third Isaiah, and of egalitarian and communal governance, are both closely related to the biblical idea of every human person as made in the image of God, and as potentially a vessel of the Holy Spirit. St Paul gave precise shape to the political implications of these beliefs in his conception of the Church as the body of Christ, adopting the image of the body from contemporary Roman political thought. But he gave a particular twist to the body metaphor, arguing in his first letter to the Corinthians that it is the presence of the Spirit in the life of every member which gives them the creative potential to participate in the common life of the Church, and hence that every member from the strongest to the weakest should have a voice and a part to play in the collective life of the community.

The early Church and many of its more radical successors, from the utopian Diggers of Gerrard Winstanley in seventeenth-century England to the members of the liberation theology base communities of contemporary Latin America, practised this vision of community participation, of leadership as service, of communal self-sufficiency and of egalitarian 'every-member ministry'. Indeed it was the recovery of this vision of a democratic and participative ecclesiastical polity in parts of Reformation Europe and North America which provided the ideological precursor to the modern ideals of a universal franchise and of civil society. Equally it was this spiritual and ethical vision of communal participation and ownership of the body politic and economic which informed the strong egalitarianism of the traditional Labour party.

The gravest danger of the drive to modernise or globalise the Labour party is that this fundamental trust in the capacity of people to govern themselves, and the egalitarian ideal which accompanies it, is suppressed in the attempt to present a united and centralised vision of what New Labour stands for behind a strong leader. There is a similar problem in relation to the effects of globalisation on the wider civil and social fabric as the forces of corporate capitalism undermine the capacity of people to achieve economic security for themselves and their families, or of local communities, cities and regions to govern and order their affairs for the welfare of their own people.

The man who inspired Tony Blair's early vision of Christian socialism, John MacMurray, in his *The Creative Society*, points out that one of the sharpest differences between communism and Christian socialism is in the attitude to leadership. Strong communist leaders incite fear in their followers as a means to secure their hold on power, and so help to paralyse constructive social activity. Christian socialists are also prone to look for strong leadership as the means to achieve their political vision. But according to MacMurray this desire is 'conspicuously anti-democratic and therefore anti-Christian'. Quoting the words of Jesus in the Gospel of Mark, 'He that would be first among you let him be your servant', and MacMurray concludes: 'it is of the first importance to remember that Christianity looks for the creative source of social integration in the common people.'[19] These words are an indictment of the cult of the leader whether of Thatcher or Blair, and the continuing centrist and anti-democratic drift of political culture in Britain which this cult has sponsored.

The mission of the Church universal has been sustained through history not by the centrifugal powers of Rome or Canterbury but by the place-based and participative character of the local congregation. Similarly a Christian political vision of the good society needs to be rooted in a belief in the creative

---

19 John MacMurray, *The Creative Society: A Study of the Relation of Christianity to Communism* (London: Student Christian Movement, 1935), 128.

power of local human communities, acting in diversity and solidarity, to construct a more participative and hence a more equal and a more just world.

14. The Global Corporation and the Body Politic

May 2003

And the multitude of them that believed were of one heart and of one soul: neither said any of them that any of the things which they possessed was their own; but they had all things common. And with great power gave the apostles witness of the resurrection of the Lord Jesus: and great grace was upon them all.

Acts 4:32–33

The Galician coast of Northern Spain has long been famed for its shellfisheries. Pilgrims to Santiago de Compostella in the Middle Ages used to be given a cockle shell which they displayed on their hats as witness to their having completed the long walk across Northern Spain to the third-most holy shrine of Christendom. Today on the Galician coast the fisherfolk are idle; the shellfish have been devastated by 17,000 tons of thick black crude oil washed ashore from the ruptured hull of the *Prestige* tanker which sank 60 miles off the Spanish coast late last month. The World Wildlife Fund in Spain estimates that thousands of sea birds have also perished, as hundreds of volunteers are still struggling to clear oil sludge from beaches and wetlands, and to rescue marine birds for treatment. The birds are unable to fly and will be suffering from hypothermia as the oil dissolves natural oils in their feathers which both keep them warm and prevent the feathers from becoming waterlogged.

The *Prestige* oil tanker was a 26-year-old single-hulled tanker owned by a Greek businessman trading through Liberia to avoid tax, and registered in the Bahamas, also to avoid tax and regulation by the authorities. The Lithuanian-originated oil was owned by a small Russian oil company – Crown Resources –

trading from an office in Central London. The owner of the company, Mikhail Fridman, is listed by *Forbes* magazine as one of the world's richest men. But it is not only wealthy Russian oil men who hire unsound ships like the *Prestige*. The big oil companies including Shell, Esso and BP regularly use these same single-hulled ships to move their own oil around the world, and it was just such a tanker – the *Exxon Valdez* – which spilt an even larger load onto the pristine and fragile coast of Alaska eight years ago, doing long-lasting damage to that region. The European Union and the United Nations both have long-term plans to phase out the use of old, rusty, single-hulled ships like the *Prestige*, but not until 2010 or, in the case of the UN, 2015. These bans come too late for the Galician Coast.

And it is not only the single-hull design which makes much of the world's fleet of oil tankers floating ecological and human time bombs. The crews on these ships, flying under flags of convenience, are mostly poorly trained and badly paid. They often cannot even communicate with each other in a common language, let alone with coastguards, tug boat captains and port authorities. Merchant mariners were among the first group of workers to experience the strictures of the new 'flexible' labour market now said to be requisite for doing business in a global economy. And the giant oil companies were among the first corporations to adopt new management methods in the 1970s which involved off-loading key activities – such as oil transportation – onto cost-cutting sub-contractors. This same 'flexibility' – long hours, poor pay, dangerous working conditions, badly maintained machinery, a ban on union activity and disregard for environmental regulations – is now endured by millions of workers in manufacturing, service and transport industries around the world as deregulated capitalism goes global.

As the United States prepares to go to war over oil, it continues a much longer war of attrition through the World Trade Organization and the International Monetary Fund, aided and abetted by the free trade zealots of the European Commission, and by global business collectives like the World Economic Forum, against the efforts of sovereign states to require corporations to pay the full social and ecological costs of their activities. The UK government is equally gung-ho in its attempts to reign back the powers of the state to regulate big business, as was evident in the failure of the government to include a promised bill on corporate killing in the recent Queen's Speech. Despite all the talk at the second Earth Summit in Johannesburg in September of corporate capitalism becoming more ecologically responsible, needing less regulation and more encouragement, the *Prestige* spill is a graphic reminder of the gap between public relations rhetoric, and the cost-cutting, cost off-loading bottom line of big corporations.

The first true corporation in Christian history was the first church in Jerusalem. It may not have owned property but it rapidly took up its responsibilities as the body of Christ when it deputed deacons to serve the poor, widows and orphans among its growing body of members, and when it shared the property of its members according to the need of each. Sometimes misdescribed as communists, the early Christians were in fact the first mutualists. They did not abolish private property, or proscribe trade by the wealthy. On the contrary the early Christians used the private houses of their wealthiest members as the first church buildings. But their ethic of mutuality involved an accountability of neighbour for neighbour, a sharing of risk and destiny, which is the complete antithesis of the sub-contracting, cost-cutting, tax-sheltering regime favoured by global corporations and their political allies.

Social arrangements which set corporations above local communities, anonymous and unregulated profit-taking above personal accountability and responsible trading, are continuing evidence of humanity's original fall from grace. For Christians the non-coercive, mutual, worshipping community, modelled on the non-competitive Trinitarian being of God, is the true form of the social. The Christian Church takes its rise from Jesus' extraordinary offer of access to God for everyone, a vision of the social which John D. Crossan describes as the 'unbrokered society'. When Christians meet together for worship they are embracing and celebrating an alternative social order of peaceable life together: not the result of human contract but the gift of the Creator.

But as citizens and consumers we also dwell in the other social, structured as it still is by sin and coercion, and in that social we buy petrol, heat houses, hold shares in pension funds invested in corporations, and elect politicians. And this is why being a neighbour in a global economy means taking every such economic and political action as a symbolic opportunity to hold investors and corporations and politicians to a higher model of responsibility than the one they are currently foisting on the global commons, and on the fisherfolk of Galicia. And this way of being a neighbour resists the efforts of government to promote a form of globalisation which reduces the capacity of communities collectively to hold corporations accountable for the human and ecological costs of their activities.

Christians from New Testament times have understood the legitimacy of government to reside in its God-given responsibility to resist sin, and to direct human affairs towards the common good. Christians then as citizens will want to dissent from the current global transfer of sovereignty from citizen groups, local authorities and regional and national assemblies to unelected and unaccountable private corporations. Hence Christian Aid and the World Development Movement are both pressing the British government to adopt a fairer and more ecologically sustainable approach to international trade than that sponsored by the World Trade Organization.

Local churches which get involved in such campaigns are giving effect to precisely the kind of image of the social which is embodied in worship of the God who is three in one. But there is a deeper way in which we as a church enact the body politic that the apostles first enacted in Jerusalem. As members of this church we collectively work together to create and maintain a community of gathering and worship, and to express mutual care and responsibility for one another as fellow members of this community. The form of our worship is a powerful enactment of the participative nature of this gathered community engaging as it does more than ten musicians, readers, intercessors, greeters and ministers in addition to the preacher and the celebrant. Worship in this church is truly presbyterian not because we lack a bishop – for indeed we have one – but because without the participation of every member we would not have the lively and engaging worship which, Sunday by Sunday, draws us here.

Participation is the key word here. The early Christians came to understand that God was in Jesus in a way God had never been in a human being before or would be since. And they also came to understand that by the gift of the Spirit which we celebrate in the Feast of Pentecost they continued to participate in that new incarnational divinity even in the absence of the living breathing presence of Jesus Christ. The gift of the Spirit enabled them to discover the truth of the godhead – the mutual participation of one God in three persons – that Christians later called Trinity, in their own gathered community. The apostles in Jerusalem did not then only preach the Gospel of the Risen Lord after Pentecost. They acted it out, they lived it, they *participated* in it when they discovered that their private possessions were also gifts from God. And hence the gift of the Spirit gave them the courage to rediscover their own property as gifts, and to put it at the disposal of the community for the mutual care of the needs of all. And it was this mutual giving of gifts which was the form of love which they had for one another and which led others to say of them, as reported later in the Acts of the Apostles, that they were 'turning the world upside down'.

Trinity

15. The Mandate of Heaven and the Divine Trinity

May 2008

The grace of the Lord Jesus Christ, the love of God, and the fellowship of the Holy Spirit be with all of you.

2 Corinthians 13:13

Some in China are saying that the 'mandate of heaven' has been withdrawn from the Chinese government after a series of disasters, natural and political, have beset the country in recent months. The tragic earthquake in Sichuan Province is the worst by far and has led to an appalling loss of life and human suffering on a terrible scale. While the government has done everything it can to respond, and has allowed foreign emergency teams in to help, members of the over-controlling Communist Party hierarchy may still recall that the great Ming Dynasty was brought down by just such a series of disasters in the seventeenth century.

Some in Myanmar are also saying that the gods are punishing the generals for their reign of terror over the compassionate and peaceable Burmese people. It is not the generals in their cocooned Rangoon mansions that are suffering but the people of the Irrawaddy Delta. And the tragedy of the loss of life and destruction of such a large area from the cyclone that hit there two weeks ago is being made so much worse by the refusal of the government either to intervene with military resources – in the way it frequently does when the Burmese protest for democracy – and provide urgent assistance to the million people displaced by the cyclone. As we all know the government is also refusing to allow foreign aid personnel into the country and tying up the large quantities of food aid that are being sent in bureaucratic obfuscation.

When the great Lisbon earthquake struck in the eighteenth century, killing tens of thousands of Portuguese, Europeans at the time said if this is the work of God then this God is not worth worshipping. The earthquake played a significant part in the turn of Europeans towards Enlightenment rationalism and now the majority of Europeans are atheists or agnostics. And even here in Malaysia we live in a culture increasingly shaped by rationalism, science and technology. And in such a culture the idea that God or the gods may be punishing these countries seems to us to be a simple superstition. These are natural events – they have nothing to do with human behaviour.

But actually this may not be far from the truth. The Chinese have built a significant number of very large hydro projects in the Sichuan province, and in areas close to it, including the contro-versial giant Yangtze dam sometimes called the Three Gorges Dam. These dams create large and very heavy bodies of water which sit on the earth's crust where before there were flowing rivers and it is well established that this causes seismic changes. And so it is quite possible – and some in China are saying this already – that the exceptional strength of this destructive earth-quake was caused by human activity and in particular the human quest to turn nature into a store of power and hence of economic value. The cyclone that hit Burma with such exceptional force is also quite likely a consequence of human activity though it must be said not of the activities of people in Burma. Scientific surveys reveal that the Indian Ocean where this storm started is two degrees Centigrade warmer than it was 30 years ago. Warmer oceans create stronger storms and these stronger storms last longer and do more damage when they reach land. And most scientists believe warmer oceans are a product of humanly caused global warming. Both of these disasters, it turns out, are quite likely to have been caused or exacerbated by human interference with earth systems.

The earth is suffering, suffering and groaning from the extent of modern human efforts to control and re-engineer earth systems to create more human wealth. It is greed and power that are the sins driving global warming and ecosystem destruction of the kind involved in gigantic dam projects, such as the Yangtze dam or the Bakun dam here in Malaysia. The Bible is quite clear about this relationship between suffering and sin. When humans pursue idols of wealth and power they create suffering for other human beings and for other creatures. And ultimately the land itself may punish humans for their sinfulness and lack of restraint, as recorded by many of the Old Testament prophets.

And yet in our reading today Christ says that 'All authority is given to me in heaven and earth' (Matt. 28:18). Whatever we may say about global warming or ecosystem destruction, these last words of Christ nonetheless give us pause – does this not mean God could have prevented these terrible disasters even if they were partly humanly caused?

But this is to seriously misread the relationship between God and creation. And it was just such a misreading which led to the atheist interpretation of the great Lisbon earthquake – God is cruel if he is God and lets this happen. But the idea of God involved in such a judgment is not the Christian idea of God but rather that of the seventeenth-century English theologian William Paley who envisaged God as a watchmaker who winds up the universe at the beginning and then leaves his workmanship to get on with things on its own. The god of the deists is an uninvolved god, a distant god, the great 'unmoved mover' unmoved by human suffering and unmoved by the groanings of creation.

For Christians this is not the God we worship because ours is the religion of the incarnation. We meet today on Trinity Sunday at the end of the great liturgies of Passiontide, Eastertide, Ascension, and Pentecost. By Trinity Sunday most preachers are getting a bit tired and wondering what on earth to say about this 'difficult' doctrine. But actually the answer to our dilemma about where is God in these natural disasters is found in the doctrine of the Trinity.

The first Christians came to experience Christ as God, as St Paul's final words to the Corinthian church – now one of our most treasured prayers – indicate. To Jews, and then to Muslims, the idea that Christ is God is offensive. Prophet or rabbi he may have been but he was not God. For if he was God then God is not One. But for the first Christians God could not be One in the old sense of only one existent form if God was in Christ as well as in the Father in heaven. There had at least to be duality in God if it was not blasphemous or idolatrous to worship Christ as God. And then after Pentecost Christians also came to know God as Spirit, present in their worship, present in their lives, bringing forth the fruits and gifts of the Spirit.

So the Christians by the second and third century began to speak openly and explicitly of God as Trinity, a word not used in the New Testament but which nonetheless is implied in this great farewell prayer of St Paul to the Christians at Corinth.

Now if God is Three and not One then we have a new way to interpret the first words of the creation story that the Spirit was present in the original waters of chaos covering the earth and the Spirit was active in the imposition of order on chaos, with the separation of darkness from light and of dry land from the water. And if the Spirit was present in the beginning, and is present in the 'new creation' which is the body of Christ, the Church, then this also helps unfold the meaning of the passage from Isaiah this morning which indicates that the Spirit of God is not only the divine driving force of creation but present and active in the cosmos as the one who sustains and holds together all that gives life and all living beings.

And if this Trinitarian interpretation of creation is true – and God as Spirit is continuously active within creation – then when the creation suffers groaning and travail as a consequence of human sinfulness, or of other sources of natural stresses on the earth system such as volcanoes and earthquakes and tsunamis, then we cannot say that God is a cruel and distant God for creating a world that has such bad events in it for God as Spirit is *within* the storm or the earthquake, and God as Spirit is with those who suffer from the storm or the earthquake. For we learn from the crucifixion of Christ that God is with those who suffer and not cruelly sitting outside of creation's groaning. This is why for us the great words of Christ's commission to go into all the nations are not just an invitation to Christian mission as discipling. They are also an invitation to be Christ's disciples, to model Christ's behaviour by healing the sick, giving food to the hungry and proclaiming and enacting justice to the oppressed. And this is why we as Christians are already actively taking steps to help in the disasters in Myanmar and Sichuan. I have been very glad to receive emails from Bishop Moon Hing of his and others' efforts both to raise money for disaster relief and to reach people in the stricken areas. And I am sure we will all want to do our part to support these valuable efforts. And this is not a distraction from Christian mission. On the contrary it is the mission of God, for God in Christ is revealed as a God of compassion, a God who intervenes, who suffers alongside, and who challenges the root causes of poverty, sickness and oppression.

The doctrine of the Trinity also helps us to understand something about the creation that in our rationalist and science-dominated culture we are in danger of forgetting: that we live in a relational cosmos, and not in a machine of unrelated atoms. God is revealed in the doctrine of the Trinity to be a God who is already a relational being before the world began. The very possibility of diversity, multiplicity and plurality in the universe arises precisely from the original Trinitarian relations of God as Father, Son and Spirit. And this also helps us to see that our dangerous interferences in the earth system – with our excessive greenhouse gas emissions and are attempts to over-control great and crucial earth systems such as large rivers – are dangerous to other creatures and to ourselves because they disrupt the relational nexus which is life-sustaining. And in this perspective when we interfere with the renewing and sustaining powers of God's creation we are not only damaging that creation – and the habitats of other creatures and even of ourselves – but we are also constraining, disrupting, undermining the Spirit of God who is active in the cosmos in the continual renewing capacities of the earth's life-sustaining powers.

So then as Christians our mission in the context of these natural disasters is first and foremost to bring relief to those who are tragically suffering in the midst of them. But we should also recognise the role of human idolatry, and the sinful lust for power and greed, in the extent of interference in the earth's systems and hence in the suffering of those who are affected by growing numbers of extreme weather events. And therefore our mission is also to seek ways together to live more sustainably on God's earth, and to find ways of living which respect rather than re-engineer the atmosphere, rivers, forests and oceans. God as Spirit is the divine engineer and unless our engineering efforts reflect and mimic the relational character of God's creative and sustaining activity then they represent not progress but regress in the unfolding of the divine plan for the creation and for human life within it.

So when we pray these great words of St Paul let us pray that the grace of the Lord Jesus Christ, which we seek to cooperate with, is a grace which recalls God's special present with the poor and the suffering – whether human or non-human – in God's creation. And when we pray for the love of God let us pray that that love will melt our hard hearts so that we love again all those creaturely forms that materially sustain our daily lives and so find ways to use the earth more respectfully and less wastefully. And when we pray for the fellowship of the Holy Spirit let us pray for the presence of the Spirit in our church communities, and beyond in our local communities and in our society so that we learn in all our human and creaturely relationships to live in peace and harmony so far as is possible with all peoples and all creatures.

> *Now to him who by the power at work within us is able to do more than all we can ask or imagine. To him be Glory in the Church and Jesus Christ throughout all ages, world without end.*

Amen

Ephesians 3:20–1

Creation Time

16. The Earth Remains Forever

September 2005

As you do not know the path of the wind, or how the body is formed in a mother's womb, so you cannot understand the work of God, the Maker of all things.

Ecclesiastes 11:5

Last year, in a tiny aeroplane, scientists flew into the eye of the tropical storm Hurricane Wilma as it straddled the Caribbean between Cuba and Mexico. Rather them than me! But they got an amazing result: their instruments measured the lowest barometric pressure ever recorded at 882 millibars.

For the first time, last year US meteorologists ran out of letters in the English alphabet with which to name hurricanes and had to turn to Greek. Of course we in academia have been using alphas and betas for a long time, though with grade inflation we rarely get to gamma these days.

It is easy to think of such hurricanes as acts of God. But a recent scientific study has found that raised sea surface temperatures in the Gulf of Mexico and the mid-Atlantic are creating anticyclones of much greater power and duration. Scientists suspect that raised ocean temperatures are a consequence of humanly generated global warming.

The book of Ecclesiastes is one of the most quoted in the Bible. It speaks to the ambiguities of life on what can sometimes seem a callous and dangerous planet. The wind blows, the rain falls, regardless of the farmer who looks up in the sky before sowing his seed in the ground; the tree falls where it is going to fall no matter who may be walking by underneath.

Today we imagine that we know far more about the world than the writer of Ecclesiastes. We know for example exactly how the body is formed in the mother's womb – scientists have created wondrous still photographs which show every stage of gestation of a human child from the first division of embryonic cells to full term. But does this increased knowledge increase our respect for pre-term children? Hardly.

British doctors in public hospitals perform more than 80,000 procedures a year to terminate the lives of perfectly healthy pre-term children. And Britain is one of a very few countries on earth which funds scientists in public hospitals to experiment on human embryos – and the HFEA last week announced an application from scientists at Kings' College London and Newcastle University to produce the first chimeric embryos which will be part human and part rabbit or goat or sheep. The intention is to use egg sacks from animals – because eggs are easier to obtain from laboratory animals – and to use human stem cells to grow human embryos inside them.

The problem, as the preacher Qoheleth, the writer of Ecclesiastes, is well aware, is that knowledge, 'the making of many books', does not equate to true wisdom. For all of our ability to peer into the womb, we still do not know whether or not an embryo has a soul. Legislators in parliament made a judgment on the matter – but they will not know if they are right or wrong until they leave their court for a higher one.

Modern technologies seem to promise control over nature, and even over our own bodies. But reading Ecclesiastes reminds us that we are still not in control of our destiny. Like the trader who sends out his wares on the water, hoping it will come back to him with profit, our lives are not in our hands.

The fatalism of Ecclesiastes – 'vanity of vanities', says the preacher, 'all is vanity' – can sometimes seem troubling. But careful exegesis reveals that this sense of the futility of life does not arise from creation itself. No – when the preacher cries 'vanity of vanities' he is speaking of the alienation humans often feel in their cosmic home. And this alienation stems not from the cosmos in its seemingly chaotic but ultimately purposeful symbiosis but from human wickedness.

When God is not at the centre of their lives then indeed there is vanity in the ways people fill their time from the writing of many books to the pursuit of beautiful women – lecturers or lecherers, take your pick – for Qoheleth both are vain. Yes, by all means, Qoheleth says, follow your desires; and especially when you are young. But be prepared to be disappointed – if you follow your desires apart from God they will not bring you true joy.

Qoheleth is a Jean-Paul Sartre of the fifth century BC. Just as Sartre announced that without God humanity is terribly alone in the universe, so Qoheleth shows us how apart from God we cannot grasp truth of life on earth.

Qoheleth is also a powerful *preparatio evangelium* – he prepares the way for Christ. As we read him we discern that without God's saving action in Christ we above all other creatures are alienated from the earth.

And the counsel of Qoheleth, like the counsel of Christ, trains us not to look for salvation in our efforts to control nature. The wisdom of his day was that those who traded their wares in ships would find meaning and purpose in their wealth. But far from it he tells us – all the riches in the world will not save you from futility, or from the dangers of a stormy earth; only when you acknowledge a higher power, and your own mortality, will you be redeemed from vanity and transformed into divinity. Even more than the ancients, we in our industrial civilisation have imagined we have acquired divine power in our ability to control nature. But instead of control over the earth industrial technologies are, quite literally, reaping the whirlwind.

In the opening chapter of this extraordinary book we find the memorable words – 'the earth remains for ever'. But we live in revolutionary times where technology changes our way of life so dramatically that we find it hard to enter imaginatively into the lives of previous generations. Equally we can hardly imagine what people's lives will be like just 50 years from now. One of the consequences of living in such a fast moving and fast changing culture is that we lose a sense of the connectedness and continuity of time. And in such a culture the urge to conserve is increasingly lost.

This is because the desire and willingness to conserve things for future generations relies on a sense of connection between present and past which the modern age destroys. As Edmund Burke wrote in his reflections on the French revolution, 'people will not look towards posterity when they fail to reflect on past generations.'

For Christians posterity and the future are deeply intertwined in the recognition that Christ is both Alpha and Omega, and that the stories of our lives only have a proper direction when they are joined to that greatest story of all, of a saviour in an ox's stall. John of Patmos in that alphabetical image of Christ as the beginning and the end recalls the prologue of St John the Evangelist in which, in the categories of the Greeks and not the Jews, he tells us that the rational faculty of the divine mind from which the world was constructed – the original and ordering logos – is the one who is born in flesh in Jesus Christ. And while most on earth are too vain, too foolish to receive him as the incarnate and cosmic Lord, those who do receive him are born again as the true children of God.

At the heart of the message of the prologue is the affirmation that even before there were Jews and Greeks, Babylonians and Egyptians, before civilisation itself began, the earth endured. And later in the same Gospel we read that 'God did not send his Son into the world to condemn the world, but that the world should be saved through him.'

The everlasting earth is redeemed from human vanity by he who is the everlasting man. And it is the everlasting man, Jesus Christ, who sustains us as we seek to persuade ourselves and our neighbours to respect and to conserve the earth which remains for ever the work of God, the maker of all things.

17. The Climate of Communion

July 2002

Woe to those who add house to house and join field to field until everywhere belongs to them and they are the sole inhabitants of the land. Yahweh Sabaoth has sworn this in my hearing: 'Many houses shall be brought to ruin, great and fine, but left untenanted; ten acres of vineyard will yield only one barrel, ten bushel of seed will yield only one bushel.'

Isaiah 5:8–10

In March this year British scientists stood on the freezing deck of the *James Clark Ross* survey ship and watched as an ice shelf the size of Kent cracked apart into thousands of giant icebergs. The break up of Larsen B, more than 220 metres thick and positioned at the Northern edge of Antarctica, is the biggest single event in the 30-year collapse of the polar ice shelves brought about by rising sea temperatures which are a consequence of global warming.

In June, Colorado saw its largest ever outbreak of wild fires threatening thousands of hectares of wilderness and residential homes, while forests in southern California, Utah, Arizona and New Mexico were also aflame after one of the driest winters on record. In Southern Africa aid agencies report that millions of people are on the verge of famine as their crops have failed for the second year in exceptional drought conditions which follow the warmest and driest decade in the region for more than a century.

The climate in many parts of the world is becoming so unpredictable that drought, flood or fire pose increasingly regular and destructive threats to some of the poorest and most populous regions of the planet. In the rich North residents and businesses are insulated by insurance, government assistance and personal or corporate wealth from the effects of climate change. But in the

South climate change and associated environmental problems are a significant cause of poverty and crop failure and a contributory factor in the current refugee crisis in Africa involving more than ten million people.

Climate change and its unequal effects on the poorest regions of the earth should be the central issues on the agenda of the forthcoming World Summit on Sustainable Development to be held in Johannesburg at the end of August. In June three thousand government and NGO representatives gathered for two weeks in Bali to prepare for this ten-year follow-up to the Earth Summit in Rio. However they were unable to agree on what should be discussed at the summit because the United States, Australia, Japan and Canada refuse to acknowledge the ecological costs of the industrial and consumption patterns of the rich North, and the link between the corporate pursuit of globalisation and the growing ecological crisis.

Instead the United States and its allies have insisted that the summit at Johannesburg endorses economic globalisation as the only viable path to 'sustainable development'. The preparatory summit text discussed at Bali urged developing countries to increase their involvement in the multilateral trading system, to encourage 'public–private' partnerships, and to deregulate their agricultural, manufacturing and service sectors as means to their achievement of sustainable economic growth. The corporate vision of economic globalisation without ecological or social restraint is presented as the only way to achieve sustainable development, with no reference to the contribution of the increased volume of international trade to global warming and biodiversity loss. As a consequence most scientists and environmentalists predict that the World Summit at Johannesburg will be a major flop with no serious targets for poverty eradication or greenhouse gas reduction even on the table for discussion.

At the Rio Earth Summit ten years ago the governments of the world laid down a radical agenda, known as Agenda 21, for moving the world's economy in a more sustainable direction, and for addressing climate change. In addition to a Treaty on Biodiversity, the International Convention on Climate Change was conceived at Rio and finalised at Kyoto in 1997. But few industrialised nations have so far signed the treaty. Under pressure to show some commitment before the Second Earth Summit, the European Union ratified the Kyoto Protocol in New York at the end of May this year. However the United States, Canada, Australia and Japan remain solid in their collective opposition to Kyoto and are refusing to sign. They have similarly opposed or significantly watered down all other major international environmental treaties, including the Basel Treaty which was meant to halt the dumping of toxic waste in Third World countries, and the Biosafety Protocol which was meant to grant countries the right to say no to genetically modified foods and seeds in the absence of scientific data about their safety.

Despite the ecological reforms outlined at the first Earth Summit, in the decade since Rio world poverty has increased, fossil fuel use has grown, thousands of novel chemicals and hundreds of genetically modified species have been released into the environment, while the destruction of the world's forests and ocean habitats – the main causes of species extinction – has continued unabated.

Biblical writers consistently view environmental disasters as the consequence of human corruption and injustice, and the failure to worship God as the generous creator of the earth. The great flood described in Genesis was seen by the authors of Genesis as the judgment of God on those who had turned the earth into a violent and wicked place. But while the people were so wretched that God virtually wiped them out, God saved the animals, birds and creeping things through the device of Noah's ark. Once the flood receded they, along with the descendants of Noah, were invited in the covenant God declared to 'abound on the earth and be fruitful and multiply' (Gen. 8:17). The ancient story teaches us that the earth suffers ecologically when human injustice abounds, but also that God desires to redeem *all* of life from sin, and not just humankind.

Like the authors of Genesis, the Hebrew Prophets also identified a connection between ecological disaster and human sin and injustice. Isaiah argued that economic injustice, and especially the greed of rich landowners who dispossessed small farmers, was responsible for the declining fertility of the soil and the ruin of farms both small and large:

> *Woe to those who add house to house and join field to field*
> *until everywhere belongs to them and they are the sole*
> *inhabitants of the land. Yahweh Sabaoth has sworn this in my*
> *hearing: 'Many houses shall be brought to ruin, great and fine,*
> *but left untenanted; ten acres of vineyard will yield only one*
> *barrel, ten bushel of seed will yield only one bushel'.*

Isaiah 5:8–10

Analogously, Jeremiah connects ecological problems in the land of Israel around the time of the Exile, including climate change and desertification, with the failure of the people of God to worship God and follow God's laws:

> *Does the snow of Lebanon vanish from the lofty crag?*
> *Do the proud waters run dry, so coolly flowing?*
> *And yet my people have forgotten me; they burn their incense to a*
> *Nothing.*
> *They have lost their footing in their ways, on the roads of former*
> *times, to walk in tortuous paths, a way unmarked.*
> *They will make their country desolate, everlastingly derided:*
> *every passer-by will be appalled at it and shake his head.*

Jeremiah 18:14–16

The prophets point to the cosmic nature of the covenant between God and the people of God. The covenant community embraced humans and non-humans, and the land itself, in a complex web of relational connections between humanity and created order which humans neglected at their peril. And so when the people of Israel worshipped God as their sovereign Lord, and modelled their lives after God's righteousness, the land and all its inhabitants prospered. But when the people neglected the covenant, worshipped that which was not the just and holy God, and where some grew wealthy and acquired great parcels of land, while others languished in poverty, then the land itself turned to desert and its non-human inhabitants also suffered. As Isaiah puts it 'the earth is mourning, withering, the heavens are pining away with the earth. The earth is defiled under its inhabitants' feet, for they have transgressed the law, violated the precept, broken the everlasting covenant. So a curse consumes the earth and its inhabitants suffer their penalty' (Isa. 24:5–6).

In the times of Israel it was kings and wealthy landowners who oppressed the people and brought about ecological destruction as they destroyed forests and over-tilled the soil to serve their greed for greater wealth. In our own time it is giant multinational corporations which drive forward the expansion of global trade and who are responsible for so much ecological destruction in both North and South. It is also corporate influence and lobbying which has seen to it that the second Earth Summit will do nothing to reduce natural resource consumption in the rich North or to eradicate poverty in the South. This is why Greenpeace and other NGOs are urging that as well as setting real and enforceable targets to stem global warming, and world poverty and reduce species extinctions, the forthcoming Johannesburg summit should tackle the issue of corporate accountability.

The Bhopal Principles on corporate accountability, which NGOs have tabled for discussion at the summit, involve the extension of corporate liability to all 'activities that cause environmental or property damage or personal injury' including 'cradle to grave responsibility for manufactured products'. And it is proposed that corporations should be liable in the courts of the country where they maintain their HQ for damage to property, biological diversity and the environment in other countries. Consistent with Principle 14 of the Rio Declaration, states should not allow multinational corporations to 'apply lower standards of operation and safety in places where health and environmental protection regimes, or their implementation, are weaker'. But the governments of the United States and the European Union, as well as Australia, Canada and Japan, are so heavily influenced by corporate lobbying that it is unlikely that such an internationally binding treaty on the responsibilities of corporations will even be discussed at Johannesburg, let alone ratified.

For those of us disabled by environmental guilt, the focus on corporate accountability in the run-up to Johannesburg is vitally significant for it highlights the crucial role of multinational corporations in ecological destruction, and in corrupting the political process both locally and globally. It is not citizen groups who lobby or hold demonstrations to have a new hypermarket, motorway, nuclear power station, or airport runway built, or an ancient forest cut down. Those who drive these environmental nightmares are corporations, often in concert with government officials. And this is why corporate accountability, and the reform of corporate law, is potentially such a powerful device for turning back the tide of global ecological destruction.

The origins of the modern economic corporation may be traced genealogically to the Pauline idea of the body – the corpus – of Christ as the distinctive polity of the Christian Church, for it was the monastic foundations of the Middle Ages which first gave legal expression to the conception of corporate action and property ownership. However it was changes in American legal practice, later followed in Europe, which paved the way for the limited liability of modern corporations to local communities and their environments. And hence it is in the legal arena that reforms must be established. Despite their claims to powerlessness in the face of globalisation, national governments still have the capacity to shape the way in which their own courts view the actions of corporations and their responsibilities and this is why the efforts of Greenpeace and other NGOs to persuade governments to change the rules of global trade and finance are so vital.

The roots of the modern corporation in the corporate life of the Church are a powerful reminder of the potential influence of spiritual communities in shaping current economic practices. In his latest book the ecologist E. O. Wilson highlights the environmental influence of American Christians, such as those in the Evangelical Environmental Network, and argues for a new coalition between science and religion in the resolution of environmental problems. However, as at the First Earth Summit, the focus in his proposed action plan is too much on biodiversity and not enough on ecological justice.

It is only by reconnecting the welfare of the economically poor with the biodiversity of their own local bioregions that it will be possible to stem the ecological devastation that the global economy is advancing and truly to turn back the tide of extinctions which is threatening the glorious diversity of God's greenhouse. And this can only be achieved by making corporations, and corrupt government officials, legally accountable for their destruction of indigenous ecological resources, so submitting economic power to legal and political restraint.

The recognition of the need to relocalise the global economy in order to redress ecological injustice and destruction finds significant resonance with the Pauline vision of the centrality of the local worshipping communities of the Church in the divine plan to redeem creation which God inaugurated in Jesus Christ (Eph. 1:7–14 and Col. 1:15–20).

The archetypal form of Christian worship from the time of the apostles until now is the proclamation of the Gospel in and through the celebration of the Eucharist. In this paradigmatic act Christians not only recall the death of the Lord Jesus until he comes again, but also anticipate the great reversal of the messianic feast when God will 'fill the hungry with good things while the rich will be sent empty away' (Luke 1:53). Bread and wine are staple foods in the Middle East and their transformation as the sacrament of the presence of Christ connects every Christian gathering around the Lord's Table with the good earth, and with local agriculturalists and purveyors of food.

The increasingly global character of the food economy is a major promoter of human and ecological injustice and of climate change. When giant food corporations purloin forests and agricultural lands for growing feed crops for Northern-produced meat, or tropical fruits for Northern tables, they both disrupt the food security of poor communities in the South and at the same time threaten local biodiversity as these communities are forced to grow their own food on marginal lands such as hillsides, wetlands or by slashing and burning forests in the wake of the logging companies. The ecological costs of flying all this food from South to North, and of freighting food between the US and

Europe and between European countries, are immense. Air travel is a major source of greenhouse gases, and the 'need' for onward transport of all this globally traded food across North America and Europe is a major source of the constant pressure from the road haulage lobby to expand the motorway network.

When we see the relationship of Eucharist and the food economy we remind ourselves of the connections between our own consumption of food and global ecological and justice issues. Food, along with housing, is for most households the largest weekly expense. If we choose to use our money to seek out local food suppliers, whether farmers' markets, organic boxes or produce which is clearly labelled as locally grown, we are making a choice which has tremendous potential for ecological change. Buying locally grown food, or growing food on allotments or in back gardens where we have access to them, are significant means by which we can begin to reverse the ecologically destructive tide of globalisation through local actions.

Christians break bread in recognition that the death and resurrection of Christ represent the defeat of the Powers and that the peace of creation and the reign of God are already breaking in as they meet together around the Lord's Table. And the Eucharist, with its echoes in other acts of eating and food production, already anticipates the praise of all peoples that the psalmists declared would be offered to God by all of life on earth as well as all its peoples at the end of time. The governments of the rich may promote the interests of corporations before people and planet, as they look like doing in Johannesburg this August. But when local worshipping communities reconnect the Eucharist with ecological justice and the food economy they announce that the corporate corruption of politics, and the corporate destruction of natural resources, can be hopefully resisted. And they give visible shape to the good news that the trouncing of the Powers that threaten life on earth by the cross and resurrection of Jesus Christ is not only a past event but one that is constantly breaking into our present reality, and especially when Christians break bread together.

18. Fishers, Salmon and Sustainable Food

October 2000

The fishers also shall mourn, and all they that cast angle into the brooks shall lament, and they that spread nets upon the waters shall languish.

Isaiah 19:8

And Jesus, walking by the sea of Galilee, saw two brethren, Simon called Peter, and Andrew his brother, casting a net into the sea: for they were fishers.

Matthew 4:18

One of the joys of living in Scotland at this time of year is to go and watch the salmon leaping up the waterfalls amidst the pine forests and rolling hills of Perthshire as they migrate from their ocean spawning grounds up Scotland's rivers in late summer and early autumn. The struggle between fish and the downward force of the water always seems an unequal one. The fish stand up out of the water in the dark swirling eddies at the bottom of the fall, waggling their tail fins fiercely and throwing themselves progressively higher up the fall until they reach the calmer waters at the top. Often on large falls seven or eight fish may be seen at once in the air, plying their way stolidly and courageously up the fall, their brown scales and fins set in relief against the vertical rush of the peaty-white water. The whole body of the salmon is pitted against the twin forces of gravity and water in motion, and the great fish throws itself upwards as though its whole being depended upon it. Often they leap part of the way up the waterfall only to get thrown down again into the whirlpools and eddies at the bottom. But eventually they make it up and their lithe majestic bodies can be seen weaving their way through rocks and rapids above the falls heading for calmer waters and pools further upstream, where, in the warmer months, they feed on Scotland's massive population of midges, and whence they and their ancestors have been travelling back and forth to the sea for thousands of years. The migration of the salmon involves an arduous trip of thousands of miles for every individual of the species. Young fish do this trip by instinct alone, following, through the internal wiring of genetic memory, the route their forebears have taken from sea to river and back again.

In other parts of Scotland today it is possible to see salmon living and dying in very different conditions. The sea lochs of the West Coast of Scotland are among the grandest scenery the British Isles have to offer. Forming deep fissures between peat- and heather-covered islands and peninsulas of glaciated granite, these lochs have been a haven for shellfish and migrant birds, and for fishing and crafting communities, for centuries past. They also provided ideal conditions for the boats of smugglers of illicit whisky, and today one of them – Holy Loch – provides deep mooring for the United Kingdom's warrior fleet of nuclear submarines with their deadly and fearsomely expensive cargo of Trident missiles.

But if you walk or drive around many of these lochs today you will see cages moored out in the deep water, with associated floats, tanks and ropes, and the occasional boat plying around the loch checking on life below. The cages are filled with farmed salmon. The wild majestic king of fish has been reduced in these Scottish sea lochs, and in Alaskan and Norwegian fjords, to the status of an intensively reared farm animal. Each cage contains more than a thousand individual salmon and at market the contents of each cage fetch many thousands of pounds, making salmon farming a highly lucrative industry.

In order for these wild fish to survive in these unnatural conditions the cages have to be regularly laced with a cocktail of chemicals, including organophosphate nerve agents and the deeply toxic dioxin. These chemicals are essential to reduce the fungal and other infections to which the caged fish are prone, and they are used to control the millions of sea lice which infest the caged salmon, and against which they have no defence in these cramped conditions. And these chemicals are bad for the health of those who eat farmed salmon, as I have learned to my cost. Indeed farmed salmon is so toxic to my body that I will never eat it again.

Twenty-five years ago salmon farming was seen as a very effective way of reviving the depressed economic fortunes of many West Highland coastal communities and much public money was pumped in by the Scottish Office to kick start the industry. Farmed salmon has become a regular and relatively cheap meal, served in a variety of guises – smoked salmon, salmon steaks, 'ready meals' of 'salmon crumble' or 'salmon chops with garlic and chives' – in supermarkets and restaurants throughout the British Isles. But these ready meals and the incomes they have generated in Highland communities have come at an environmental price. Scotland's sea lochs are now polluted with the chemical wash from the salmon cages, and, as traditional salmon fishermen have always predicted, wild salmon are now at risk from this West coast rush for the red gold of salmon flesh.

A considerable proportion of the caged salmon in Scotland's fish farms – around 50 per cent according to some estimates – are now infected with a deadly new virus, infectious salmon anaemia, which first emerged on fish farms in British Columbia and Norway and is now affecting many farms in Shetlands and the West of Scotland. The virus renders the fish unsafe to eat and eventually kills them in very large numbers. The virus is a notifiable disease, is highly infectious and all fish stocks are killed on those farms which notify. There are fears that this virus, because it has mutated in the unnatural environment of the fish farms, will pose a threat to the wild salmon which will have no resistance against it, just as wild salmon have already been affected by the increased incidence of sea lice and other pests emanating from the farms. The first wild salmon to have caught ISA have already been discovered in a river in New Brunswick in Canada.

Salmon farming is only one of a number of government-subsidised projects which form part of the continuing quest for cheap food and which is driven by agricultural experts, scientists and government agencies. Environmental costs and animal welfare problems have been discounted for decades by the enormous output subsidies available to farmers adopting intensive rearing methods. Salmonella still infests a third of the British battery chicken stock, and BSE is now rampant not just in Britain – where its incidence is considerably lower than it has been for fifteen years – but in North America and continental Europe as well, though farmers give it different names: French farmers call it *la vache tremblante* and regularly send cows with this condition to market for slaughter. The global industry which is modern food production learns no lessons from these disasters. Constantly struggling against the natural and ecological limits of animals, land and water, agricultural scientists, supermarket managers and farmers continue to drive down the cost of food and to increase output per animal and per hectare.

The latest weapon in the arsenal of industrial techniques applied to farming in the last fifty years is genetic engineering. Genetic engineering is hailed by biotechnology companies and scientists as the answer to many of the environmental problems of modern industrial farming. Instead of using hosts of herbicides it is possible with GM crops such as Roundup Ready soya to use just one targeted herbicide, albeit in multiple and liberal applications.[20] With other crops, such as BT Cotton, it has been possible to introduce a toxin into the plant itself which kills pests – the stem borer in the case of cotton – and this obviates the need for pesticide sprays.

Scientists working for a US firm, AF Protein, on Prince Edward Island in Canada recently announced that they had successfully developed a new genetically modified salmon which grows up to ten times faster than its non-GM cousin, and over its shorter lifespan consumes 40 per cent less food. Scientists have introduced novel genes from other fish into Atlantic salmon such

---

20 See further Richard Hines and Clare Oxborrow, 'Who benefits from GM crops? The rise in pesticide use', *Pesticide News*, 79 (March 2008), 8–9.

that they express growth hormones at a higher rate, and over a much larger proportion of their body mass than non-engineered salmon. These new GM salmon achieve body mass five times faster than unmodified salmon after 18 months. GM salmon will more than halve the cost of bringing farmed salmon to market, and their introduction will also reduce the quantity of chemicals per unit of salmon in the ocean as the new genus of salmon will spend less time in the water before being harvested.

Against those who find GM salmon unnatural the scientists argue they have modified only one millionth of the genetic code of the fish, and moreover they point out that the new genes they have introduced are themselves derived from edible fish. Ergo, these fish represent no toxicological threat to humans, and their faster growing times and lower food requirements will reduce the environmental impacts of fish farming.

However another scientific report, published in 2000, emanating from Purdue University, Indiana, found evidence that fish which are genetically modified to be of larger size are more successful in reproduction when mixed with unmodified fish in a tank. This is because females instinctively identify large size with better reproductive chances and the unmodified fish therefore have fewer mating opportunities. However the offspring of genetically modified fish have lower life chances than their unmodified cousins because GM fish like other GM species such as GM sheep are less naturally robust than their non-GM counterparts. As a consequence the scientists in Indiana estimate that when GM fish escape into the wild and mate with unmodified fish, within 37 generations that species will become extinct.

Against the argument that GM salmon will ultimately wipe out wild salmon, the GM salmon scientists argue that they are designing their GM salmon so that they express the growth hormone at a stage subsequent to the reproductive cycle and so this problem will not affect GM salmon. They also claim that all their GM salmon are modified so that they are infertile and hence, even if they do escape into the wild, they will represent no long-term threat to wild species.

But wild salmon fishermen are not reassured by these counter-claims, any more than they believed earlier reassurances given by scientists and investors promoting farmed salmon more than two decades ago. No sooner have farmed salmon begun to threaten the very survival of wild salmon in Scotland than scientists and fish farmers now propose to introduce a new species of farmed salmon which, when they escape into the wild as some inevitably must, will lead to the extinction of wild salmon within thirty or forty years. The claim that all GM salmon are infertile is not reassuring as it will be impossible to guarantee infertility in an industry which artificially spawns millions of salmon every year.

The industry-friendly Food and Drug Administration of the United States Government looks set to approve the introduction of GM salmon into fish farms in Alaska and Washington State within twelve months. North American farmed GM salmon will represent a considerable cost advantage against non-GM salmon produced in other markets, including Europe where there is more resistance to this novel technology. But eventually there will be pressure – through the World Trade Organization, through commercial food producers anxious to introduce lowest-cost commodities across global markets – to adopt the GM salmon here. And in fifty years we may be able to tell our grandchildren about how the salmon once leaped in the falls below Pitlochry but we may no longer be able to show them. Cheap farmed salmon will still be available to eat, no doubt. But the oceans and the landscape will be a poorer place without the majestic king of fish.

Jesus calls fishermen as his first disciples and promises they will become 'fishers of men'. Over time the commitment of Christians to men, and women, fishing for souls was such that the Gospel of freedom and justice overtook much of Mediterranean Europe by the Middle Ages. And as its influence spread so did progress in the human condition, and in particular improvements in the human diet that saw people eating fish on a regular basis. Most of this fish was however not caught in the oceans but grown in ponds by monks. Fisherfolk mostly confined themselves to coastal waters until the invention of the navigational aids, and large watertight ocean-going ships of the late Middle Ages. Hence the monks who farmed the fish relied not on industrially trawled small fry to feed the fish but on cereals harvested from monastic lands and received as tithes.

Like so much of the modern world, modern chemical fish farming is a heretical simulacrum of a Christian practice that has long since ceased to be sustainable or just in the way it treats the creation and God's creatures. Similarly the global economy in which our acts of food purchasing are increasingly mediated represents a counter-communion to the Communion of Saints even although the existence of a global economy would not have been possible without the prior formation of a Christian civilisation in which communion between Christian citizens and merchants in distant places became an ecclesial, and hence an economic, reality.

And this is why it is significant that we continue to meet Sunday by Sunday as Christians around the table of the Eucharist. Eucharistic fellowship is of particular significance to salmon farming, and to the larger global and local food economy. For the distinctive meal of the Eucharist impacts in significant ways on all other human acts of eating and drinking in that it trains us as Christians to receive the creatures that sustain us as gifts of God, and not merely natural resources. And hence, instead of regarding the Eucharist as a 'religious' meal, and meals in the home, or shared meals at church, as non-religious, we might view all actions involving the production, sale, preparation, cooking and consumption of food as significant for the Christian witness to the Powers which direct the global food economy. The following words, used in some contemporary liturgies, when bread and wine are first taken by the celebrant, make clear the connection between Eucharistic eating and drinking and the daily production of food:

> Blessed are you Lord God of All Creation. Through your goodness we have this bread to offer which earth has

given and human hands have made. It will become for
us the bread of life.
Blessed be God for ever.[21]

Bread and wine were and are paradigmatic foods in the Middle
East and these words point to one of the core meanings of the
Eucharist as symbol of the abundance of God's redeemed creation, and of the role of good earth and good work in realising
that abundance in the form of food to sustain the human
community. Eucharistic feasting calls to mind, and sanctifies,
other acts of human work on the land, of human food production, of human eating and feasting. And participation in this feast
trains us as Christian citizens, to be discerning about the ways in
which our food is grown and marketed and to endeavour, where
we can, to eat justly and responsibly, and not just according to the
dictates of price. Of course farmed salmon is cheap. But at what
cost is this cheapness won?

---

21 *Scottish Liturgy 1982* (Edinburgh: Scottish Episcopal Church, 1982).

St Francistide

19. The Original Environmentalist?

October 2002

St Francis has been adopted as the patron saint of the environmental movement by the World Wildlife Fund. And two gatherings of world religious leaders on the environmental crisis have been held at Assisi. But how did Francis qualify for such adoption?

In the city of Saburniano, his powerful preaching had inspired all the people there to join his movement (and where he invited them to join his Third Order for they could not all leave their homes and wander around in poverty as he did). We read in *The Little Flowers of Saint Francis* how he left Saburniano – where even the swallows had fallen silent at his invitation during his preaching – and in that same fervour of spirit he journeyed on and came upon a forest where the trees were full of thousands of birds and he said to his companions 'tarry here by the way while I go and preach to my sisters the birds'. As he began preaching the birds apparently left the trees and came and stood in their thousands around the saint, and appeared to listen to his words.

> My little sisters the birds, he told them, you are
> beholden to God your creator, and always and in every
> place you ought to praise Him for he has given you
> many gifts: freedom to fly wherever you will, the air
> which sustains you in flight, the rivers and fountains for
> your drink, the mountains and valleys for a refuge, and
> the tall trees where you can build your nests and tend
> your young. And just as you cannot spin or sew God
> clothes you and your children: wherefore your Creator
> loveth you much, since He hath dealt bounteously with

you; and therefore beware, little sisters of mine, of the sin of ingratitude, but ever strive to praise God.[22]

As St Francis preached to them the birds opened their beaks, stretched their necks, and spread their wings, appearing to bow to the ground, in joyful recognition of Francis' words. And when he had finished they all took to flight in song and even their flight seemed to be inspired taking the form of a cross.

Like so much of the life of St Francis this account from *The Little Flowers* is no doubt highly embellished but the intuitions are surely Francis' and they are three. And they make a pretty good summation of a Christian ecological spirituality:

- Everything created is a gift of God and God wills its good.
- We share with all living beings in the giftedness of creation and we share in the divine care and compassion for all beings on the earth.
- With all living beings we are called to express gratitude and praise and love constantly for the gift of creation in a natural symphony of praise.

So let's take these in order. Everything created is a gift of God and God wills its good. We are the first generations of peoples on the earth to live our lives by another account of our origins. In this account the earth is not a gift from God but a chance occurrence in the history of a galaxy billions of years old. The idea of creation – that everything is ordered according to the purposes of a good and wise and loving Creator – is eclipsed by this powerful modern ideology of chance, of randomness, of creation by statistical event rather than by providential act. And if it is not created by a good God, then it is not good – instead it is ours for the remaking, to make it better. We do not respect or treat with awe and wonder a world which occurred by chance. We may even believe we are its supreme being, the highest form of consciousness. In which case it becomes our right, our privilege, even our duty, to remake the earth in our image, to engineer and consume the resources of the earth to serve our own expanding consciousness and comfort.

Life as gift – the birth of a child, serious illness, a sudden change in life circumstances can bring home to us in fresh ways

---

22   Ungolino di Monte Santa Maria, *The Little Flowers of Saint Francis* (London: J. M. Dent and Sons, 1910), 45.

the spiritual experience of life as gift. I recently got a nasty and extremely debilitating virus in California where I was working in the winter and in the midst of it I felt so weak I really wondered if I would recover. Well I did and here I am. But for some months afterwards I had this incredible sense of wonderment that I was still here, life is still for me to live. The newness, the freshness, the surprise of life – it came to me again and again. Wonder is a great gift. Richard Dawkins, the atheist evolutionary biologist and professor of the public understanding of science in Oxford, laments that science is not very good at generating wonder. The Psalms though are full of wonder, wonder at the creation of man who is made a little lower than the angels, wonder at the care of God for creation, making a space for the land between the seas and keeping it safe from inundation. The gospels too – when Jesus walked on the waters and then quelled the storm in the boat the disciples marvelled and declared he was the Son of God for even the wind and sea obeyed him. They also marvelled at the clarity and simplicity and prophetic power of his teaching, and at his many healing miracles. Signs and wonders were also the acted parables which accompanied the first preaching of the Gospel.

Our own culture devotes itself to human wonders – planes that fly higher and faster, balloons reaching up to space and down again, the pyramids, even Salisbury Cathedral. But the greatest wonders are not human made but God made – the human eye is an incredibly wondrous organ; the antennae which guide thousands of bats in and out of large cathedral-like caves in great waves in the night without ever colliding with each other; the memory of an elephant that returns year after year to the place where a parent elephant died; the extraordinary intelligence, exuberance and communicative skills of dolphins.

I want to suggest that we practise a spiritual exercise in relation to this recognition of the wondrous gift of life. The exercise is one that we can do anywhere though ideally it will be in a quiet room or on a good day in a quiet space outside. It involves imagining a wild place that you have visited and perhaps occasionally frequent in memory – a favourite river, glen or waterfall, a mountain place, coastline or wetland. Wilderness is wondrous because it mediates the beauty of creation, the difference of habitats not designed by humans, the communities of species that thrive where the absence of human agriculture or dwellings, roads or offices give them space to be. I want you to imagine this place with all the senses – taste the air as you slowly breathe in and out and let the peace of this wild place slow you down; touch the bark of a tree, the running water, the lush grass; see the delicate wing of a butterfly, the place and the vista which surrounds it; smell the grasses, the soil, the lifeblood pulsing through the species which inhabit it; listen to their noises, their sounds, songs, movements. As you imagine with the senses imagine this place as a place of divine epiphany, of divine presence perhaps recalling the first words of the Lord's Prayer and their true meaning – Our Father, you are all around us … hallowed be your name, hallowed is this place … your will be done for the earth … your will for life in all its abundance and diversity and giftedness.

The second part of Francis' teaching is that we share with all beings in this providential ordering, in experiencing the creation as gift and promise, enjoying its freedom under God. Our culture trains us to forget that we *are* our environment; that the food we eat, the water we drink, the air we breathe, actually come to constitute our very cells and bodies. Modern urban life and its mechanical dependencies and rhythms hide from us the truth of our physical dependence on the earth. Modern farmers in many places are draining the water from subterranean aquifers, the deposit of thousands of years of rain, to water hybrid seeds fed by artificial nitrogen that require a high water input. Similarly they create enormous fields where topsoil is regularly removed in harvesting. Added to soil erosion and excess water use, modern farming is destroying the worms and other insects and the birds which feed on them. Were St Francis to go into the fields of East Lothian today he would not have to silence the birds first – sadly the corncrake, the swallow, the wood pigeon and the tit are so dwindling in numbers that he would have had no competition from their collective song.

The second spiritual exercise I want to commend to you is rather like the ecologist John Seed's account of the Council of Beings in his little book *Thinking Like a Mountain*.[23] In this exercise the key is to identify with the sadness of the earth and its peoples, to deal with our own guilt, and find the compassion of God for all creation which God showed in the passion and the crucifixion of Jesus on the holy tree of Calvary. In your imaginative prayer enter into an identification with the disappearing birds, the logged forest, the destroyed coral reef, the orangutan with no space left to forage, the indigenous tribal parent with no clean rivers to fish for her children's supper. Take up an image in your mind of one particular being who has suffered from ecological destruction – it might be a person or it might be a mammal or a bird, a tree or a reptile, or even a forest glade or lowland spring, perhaps even an urban river boxed in by concrete walls. Hear the cry of despair – speak the words that come and express with them what has happened to the extinct wolf or ape or frog, the logged forest, the polluted river, the mined valley, the salty farmland; see, own and confess the sin which has given rise to this destruction; recollect the wounds of Christ who gave up his life to reconcile the whole world to God and to redeem all created order from sin; imagine the world made new, restored after the pattern and image of the wondrous reordering of life which was the resurrection of Jesus Christ from the dead and which is the promise of the new heaven and a new earth where even the lion and the lamb will lie down together. Pray for the peace of the earth, for God to have compassion on the false needs which project us to destroy her, for God to forgive our ecological and relational sins against the earth and one another; petition God to help us to recover our true need for God from our false needs for excess or luxury or distraction, ask God the Holy Spirit to fill our hearts with love and compassion for the earth and with passion to resist earth's destruction.

The third principle Francis teaches is that we are to express gratitude and praise constantly for the gift of creation. The zeal

---

23 John Seed, Joanne Macy, Pat Flemming and Arne Naess, *Thinking Like a Mountain: Towards a Council of All Beings* (Gabriola Island: New Society Publ., 1988).

which fired St Francis to leave his wealthy family and to found his order of poverty was above all a holy fire of love for the Lord Jesus Christ. Viewed apart from his love for Jesus of Nazareth, risen and ascended to be revealed as Lord of the universe, Francis' life was seen by his parents as reckless and prodigal in the extreme. And for Francis no sacrifice was too great, no act of dedicated service too extravagant, and no form of devotion too extreme for the love he held for his Lord. When he and his sister Clare – who followed Francis into the friary and went on to found a religious order for women known as the Poor Clares – got together over a meal and fell into discussing their love for their Lord, *The Little Flowers* tells how he fell into such a holy reverie that the church of St Mary's and the friary where they met to eat seemed to the people of Assisi to be on fire.

We also read how towards the end of his life Francis' body began to show the stigmata – the signs of the wounds of his Lord. Such devotion to the Lord in our age seems an incomprehensible thing. But in his love for Christ Francis embraced a life of poverty, a simplicity which was also joyful, and a humility of soul. And Francis also founded a great movement, of the Franciscans, some of whom are with us here today. And at the Reformation in England and Scotland, when the older established orders were judged corrupted by wealth and power, it was the friars of St Francis who were often found still to be keeping to the faith of simplicity and to their vows of poverty, chastity and obedi-ence, and hence to provide an enduring source of spiritual guidance and teaching to the people. Here in Scotland, as John Knox describes in his *History of the Reformation in Scotland*, a number of friars were particularly prominent around the time of the Reformation, preaching eloquently of the need for ecclesias-tical reform.

People in our age too sense the need for reform and renewal. They know there is more to life than what they possess. But the icons of our civilisation mislead them as to the true source of self-transcendence – tramping along Princes Street, or around one of the new cathedral-like malls springing up in all our Western cities as temples to the alchemy of shopping. The powerful marketing of brands and consumer goods train them to imagine they will find their true self – expressed in this dress, that jacket, or the other fragrance. These goods are marketed with a promise – they will make us whole, enable us to transcend our identity among the masses, to emulate the celebrity rich who are in our imagination before we ever made the purchase.

Instead of want Francis teaches us of the danger of ingratitude – once we forget that the world is the good gift of God, we abuse it. And this idea is not Francis' alone. The first commandment teaches that if we set up any created thing in the place of our love and devotion to God we will frustrate our own good and the good of other creatures. The collective neglect of this first and great commandment has been the occasion of an unprecedented global holocaust of species which are becoming extinct at a speed of attrition unknown in human history.

Love, praise, gratitude for the wonder of being, all beings, expressed in extravagant, joyful, transcendent acts of devotion to their Creator: it is these which we see in the life of St Francis. And might these not also transform our world, and ourselves, from the mad and reckless quest for material satisfaction and supervenience through consumerism? To be this-worldly in a way which cares for the world we need to be other-worldly; to find ourselves in transcendence, not of having but of being, not of possessing but of being possessed; not in consuming but in being consumed by love for God. This love we are invited to discover again and again: in the divine meal prepared for us in the sanctuary, in the saying of the Psalm early in the morning, or in the wonderful effortlessness of the lone buzzard hovering in the updraft on the wing as we walk in the fields the Lord made for us to experience a glimpse of his divine majesty and freedom and grace.

And so to the third and final spiritual exercise I commend to you. In Jesus Christ, resurrected and ascended, God invites us to participate in the new creation which he has determined for us and for all life. The form of our participation in the new creation is pneumatological. It is the divine Spirit who enables the disciples after the Ascension to experience and express the life transforming grace of the power of the resurrection in their lives and worship and witness. In place of the icons of our civilisation we need the power of the true icon – the true image of the invisible God in the face of Jesus Christ. I suggest that you might find such an icon in a magazine or book, or perhaps in a religious bookstore, and place it somewhere in a small opening or on a small wall in your house. Set a candle in front of it. And as night falls light the candle, and as you do so direct your prayer to God the Holy Trinity with the help of the image of Christ incarnate, made flesh, and whose Spirit remains as the token of his enduring presence. Pray this time with your eyes open. Address and repeat a few times the hallowed words of the Jesus prayer to Christ in the Spirit: 'Lord Jesus Christ, Son of God, Have Mercy on Me a Sinner.' And so recall the humility and the devotion of Francis, not only the patron saint of ecology but the devoted servant of the Creator of all being, and the One in whom all things hold together, in the flesh and in the Spirit.

Ordinary Time

20. Hospitality and the Great Game

October 2001

There was a certain rich man, which was clothed in purple and fine linen, and fared sumptuously every day: and there was a certain beggar named Lazarus, which was laid at his gate, full of sores.

Luke 16:19–20

I have never lived in the Middle East but so many of the gospel stories and parables depend upon some knowledge of the cultures of that region that I think maybe it is time I went. The nearest I came to having a sense of being there was strangely enough in London one hot summer in the late 1970s. Now London is a city I think that I know, since I am from there. But when my wife's sister married an Iranian, and we visited with them for a week, I discovered another, Iranian London, which was completely different from the one I knew. Apart from the visits to unfamiliar places where Iranians tended to stay – Kilburn, Notting Hill – and the meals of saffron-scented lamb and Iranian rice, eaten seated on Persian rugs on the floor high up in an apartment block in West London or a Notting Hill flat, my strongest memory is of the hospitableness of Iranian friends and relatives, and their frequent invitations to come and stay with them in their homes in Iran, which were wholly genuine. We often thought of following up on these offers. We even dreamt of an overland odyssey in our old Morris Oxford, though we never made it, and I suspect the car would have expired long before Istanbul, let alone Tehran.

Hospitality is fundamental to the cultures of the Middle East. And this is partly a matter of geography as well as custom. These countries are for the most part very sparsely populated, they are very hot, and ground water is scarce. And when people travel from place to place – and many followed a nomadic lifestyle for some months of the year with their animals – they are accustomed to offering hospitality to those few that they meet on the way, and to receiving it in turn. And sometimes such offers can be a matter of life or death. It is not surprising then that so many of the gospel stories and parables relate to meals and invitations to share them, and to those who were excluded from them, such as the poor man Lazarus from the table of Dives.

The details of this parable are fairly striking and worth dwelling on before we go further. First we should note that Dives was seriously rich. He lived in a large palatial residence and we know this because the word translated gate – puw'na – actually refers to a high ornamented portico. Lazarus on the other hand was too ill even to reach the basket of bread which was thrown to the dogs after the meal and which the rich traditionally used as napkins to mop up during their lavish feasts. Lazarus dies without ceremony – perhaps the dogs ate from his bones – but he goes straight to heaven so he must have been a righteous man. Dives dies, much later, and is properly buried. But after their deaths their fortunes are starkly reversed and while Dives is in hell, Lazarus enjoys intimacy with Abraham himself.

This reversal of fortunes would have been deeply worrying, even offensive, to Jesus' hearers who were those same Pharisees who had been so offended at the Parable of the Unjust Steward. The Pharisees believed that wealth comes to the rich as a reward from God for their righteousness and obedience to the law, a belief that has some scriptural foundations in the books of Deuteronomy and Proverbs.

The parable though is not a simple condemnation of the wealthy, not least because we know that Abraham himself was a very wealthy man. The point about Dives is that he used his wealth entirely for self-centred enjoyment and personal gain. He was uninterested in the dire state of the beggars on his street, too caught up in his own revelries to notice the illness and malnourishment of the poor beyond his gated palace. Dives' sin was his failure of compassion and it is for this failure, not for his wealth per se, that he languished in torment even as his five brothers were gathered in their father's house for the wake after his last rites.

Jesus lived in Palestine at a time when failures of compassion had become commonplace. Israelite society had traditionally been ordered by the law in such a way as to minimise the kind of extremes of poverty and wealth that the parable displays. Regular debt forgiveness was enshrined in the law according to the Sabbath and Jubilee laws as described in Leviticus. These laws had the intent of preventing great extremes of wealth in Israel. And they were also intended to restrict bonded labour and slavery so that the people of Israel did not become homeless slaves as their ancestors had been in the land of Egypt. They represent in effect what ecological economist Herman Daly calls the 'eleventh commandment'. But under the duress of Roman law and Roman taxes, the traditional organisation of Israelite society was breaking down. Many smallholders and farmers were driven into debt by excessive taxation while a small elite of Jewish money lenders and religious leaders became very wealthy as they bought up the lands and small enterprises of their less fortunate neighbours. It is in this context that we should read both the Parable of the Unjust Steward and the Parable of Dives and Lazarus. Jesus is not condemning people enjoying the occasional feast, or even people who live in large houses. After all the early Church for whom Luke wrote this gospel relied on precisely such people for it was they whose homes were large enough to allow the members of the first house churches to meet together in one place on the Lord's Day. No, his teaching is directed against the wealthy and religious elites who used the occupation of Israel by the Romans to become wealthy while the poor were becoming destitute. The story is a story of judgment for those who collaborated with the powers of domination that oppressed the ordinary people of Israel, and it is a story of liberation for those people who were being excluded in ever larger numbers from a fair share of the goods that their land had to offer.

And it was a message of liberation not only for those who first heard this story from Jesus' lips, but also for the members of those house churches where the Gospel of Luke was first circulated and read. The Gospel of Luke was written after the destruction of the temple in Jerusalem by the Romans, and hence at a time when the Pharisees had become the leaders of universal Judaism. And the Pharisees it was who began to eject all Jewish Christians from the Synagogues, and hence from the Jewish community, after the destruction of the temple. And this meant that the Jewish Christians became doubly poor. Not only were they isolated from Roman society as Jews, who were themselves looked down on by Romans. But they were excluded religiously, and there-fore economically, from Jewish society as well.

For the first hearers of this story, Jews in Palestine and Jewish Christians at the end of the first century, the striking reversal of fortune in death, when Lazarus went to heaven and Dives to hell, would have been a heart-warming and encouraging tale. They might have been suffering as the poor and excluded of the earth, but when they died and went to heaven, they would be received at the feast table in the kingdom, they would lie at the feet of Abraham himself, while their oppressors, the Romans and their Jewish collaborators, would languish in hell.

How do we hear this parable today though? I guess for most of us it is a parable that makes us feel pretty uncomfortable. We are accustomed to the fact that so far as the world as a whole goes most of us here in church can be described as relatively wealthy, at least in monetary terms. We may not all live in large houses, our gates may not be made of marble and have classical plinths on top of them, but we will have seen images of people in distant lands, or closer to home, who live in cardboard boxes and sleep under sheets of newspaper. We may even pass such people on our way to work in the morning from time to time. But feeling guilty about our relative security, and their relative poverty, will do neither them nor us any good. Guilt of this kind can actually be debilitating, disempowering. The point of this parable, and of the Parable of the Unjust Steward that precedes it, is that there is hope even for the rich, and not just for the poor. Remember what Jesus said to the Pharisees in the earlier parable: 'make friends for yourselves by means of dishonest wealth so that when it is gone, they may welcome you into their eternal homes' (Luke 16:9).

The nineteenth-century French philosopher Proudhon famously said 'all property is theft', and Marx took up the refrain. And Jesus here would seem to be saying something pretty similar. Wealth in the time of Jesus was also dishonestly gained. The debt economy – which was against the revealed law of God – produced many paupers and the wealth of the few relied on the pauperisation of the many. Is wealth any different today? How did Edinburgh get to be such a fine city? Much of the wealth of Edinburgh, like that of Liverpool, Manchester, Glasgow and London, came from the British Empire that so many Scots served so faithfully for many generations. Our cities became wealthy at the expense of the peasants of India and Pakistan, of slaves from West Africa, 'coolies' in the West Indies and Malaya, and tribes in Eastern and Southern Africa. Their lands, and often their labour too, were forcibly taken from them and the surplus value transferred to subsidise the astonishingly wealthy lifestyles of those princes, aristocrats and industrialists who inhabited the great houses of Europe in the nineteenth and early twentieth centuries, and whose luxurious remnants can still be seen in palatial houses around Edinburgh at Hopetoun and Dalmeny, Holyrood and Prestonfield. These great houses were built, like the great investment banks and stockbroker firms of our own day, and the Dockland penthouses and Tuscan villas of their managers, on coercively accumulated wealth. The Western powers may no longer have an Empire, but through military and diplomatic and economic strength, the nations of the West continue to extract vast surpluses from the oceans and forests, the sweatshops and the plantations of the Southern hemisphere. The difference though is that it is now possible, in a way it was not in the nineteenth century, for the poor from the South to get to the North, as refugees or migrants, or even as terrorists coming to wreak their revenge on those they see as their oppressors.

And this is why the events of the last few weeks are so startling, and do indeed represent a new point in our own history. In the past our nation, and our allies, could extract wealth from distant lands with no fear of consequences. Europe was never bombed by Indians or Africans. We did all the killing to ourselves on this continent. And similarly North America has never until now been bombed by any outside agent, unless you count Hawaii, which is a relatively recent colonial acquisition two thousand miles from the American continent. The difference now is that the very same technologies which have enabled the powerful to extract dishonest wealth from distant lands, with the aid of military might, have now brought a threat to this might in its heartland.

Now as soon as one says something like that there are those who will say I am justifying these terrible and tragic events. And let me say straight away that nothing is further from my mind. These were evil acts committed by people who had no interest in helping the poor. They are religious fanatics and in their world-view none but the righteous – the most zealous followers of Mohammad – have a right to life. All others, even all other Muslims, are apostates and infidels to these people and deserving of a violent death. But having once said that we must ask about the roots of religious extremism of this kind. And it becomes clear once we examine its roots that it has arisen in nations – Palestine, Saudi Arabia, India, Egypt, Pakistan, and Afghanistan – which have been pawns in the West's great game for more than two hundred years, and which are still pawns even today as the West, and especially the United States of America, continues to identify its economic security with access to cheap oil and natural gas, never mind how evil and corrupt the governments who keep selling it cheap.

Most of the terrorists who attacked New York and Washington, DC last month were Saudis. It was also Saudis who trained, supported and funded the Taliban in Afghanistan. And it is Saudi money that continues to fund Islamist maddrassas – the only available schools in many places in Pakistan and Afghanistan where future generations of children are trained in extremist Wahabbi Islam. Wahabbi Islam, which is the religious cult of the ruling family of Saudi Arabia, acts as a ritual veil that shrouds the deep rifts and injustices on which Saudi society is constructed. And Saudi oil wealth is used to spread and sponsor Wahabbi Islamic extremism to many other parts of the globe. But Saudi Arabia is seen as a friend of the West. Saudis had special access to the USA and their princes and arms and oil dealers are frequent visitors, and increasingly owners, of the grand houses and royal palaces of England and Scotland. This is not some distant inexplicable menace. Our government has been selling vast quantities of arms to these people for a very long time – so long as they keep the price of oil down we don't mind what they do to their own people.

The problem in international relations in our own times is not so different from the problem with the Roman Empire at the time of Jesus. The difference, until recently, was that, unlike in Jesus' Palestine, the victors and the victims did not live in the same streets. Dives in the colonial world was thousands of miles away from Lazarus. And though Dives might have feared the fires of hell, Lazarus presented no real threat. But those of us who have been campaigning for a long time for economic justice between rich and poor nations – by campaigning for debt relief for poor countries, by buying fairly traded goods, by supporting aid charities – have also been saying for a long time that because of the global nature of the economy, because there are oranges and grapefruit grown on land stolen from Palestinians in Tesco today, footballs made by child slaves in Pakistan at the local mall, and shirts on the high street made by sweatshop workers locked in their factories for 15 hours a day and paid less than one dollar a day, because of these things, rich Dives and poor Lazarus do now live in the same global neighbourhood.

It comes down in the end to the challenge of compassion, of fellow feeling. We will have to make some sacrifices to make the world a more economically just place. We have to pay more for clothes made by people on decent wages from materials that don't poison the earth, and for oil and gas sold at a price reflecting their scarcity and their climate-changing effects, just as we do for fairly traded coffee or tea or chocolate. Jesus in this parable is not saying to us we have to abandon our solid flats and houses and go and live on the streets. He is not saying to give up our day jobs and stop earning money to buy food and clothes. St Paul took a job to pay his way. Jesus is not asking us to feel guilty about our relative wealth in the global North as compared to the global South. But he calls us today to have compassion, to have fellow feeling, and to act on that fellow feeling, to use our wealth to work for justice for those who do not have the good things we have, but who are our neighbours in the global village.

I was much encouraged this week to see the Foreign Secretary Jack Straw experiencing some of that Iranian hospitality I got to know in London twenty years ago. I was also encouraged to hear that Jack Straw had written in an Iranian newspaper about the oppressed people of Palestine, whose olive groves, vineyards and even houses have been stolen from them by religious extremists, many of whom are from the United States, and described as 'settlers' in our newspapers.

When we begin to address the roots of hate by having compassion, by offering hospitality to economic refugees, by taking special care to be neighbour to the Muslims who live around us, and by working for justice for those whom the global economy makes our neighbours, then we are beginning to address the roots of terror. Consigning our enemies to a hell of hate and vengeance will not bring peace. Inviting them to share from our table will.

21. Bowling Alone

There is one alone, and there is not a second; yea, he hath neither child nor brother: yet is there no end of all his labour; neither is his eye satisfied with riches; neither saith he, For whom do I labour, and bereave my soul of good? This is also vanity, yea, it is a sore travail. Two are better than one; because they have a good reward for their labour. For if they fall, the one will lift up his fellow: but woe to him that is alone when he falleth; for he hath not another to help him up. Again, if two lie together, then they have heat: but how can one be warm alone?

Ecclesiastes 4:10–11

And who is my neighbour?

Luke 10:29

I was driving back one Sunday evening from the Huntingdon Museum Gardens in Pasadena to Claremont where I was teaching and writing last winter. Friends had taken me to the gardens after lunch, and they are wonderful; we saw a whole hillside of cacti coming into bloom and other areas were lush with tropical palms, or more austere with English roses, Chinese magnolia and, most memorable of all, a Japanese Zen garden complete with temple. On the 12-lane freeway between LA and Palm Springs I looked around me and began to realise as I was driving along in an empty car that this was true for 90 per cent of the vehicles around me. I was surrounded by individuals in their cars 'bowling alone', to quote the title of Robert Bellah's book about modern-day America. It was strange to me coming from Britain to see so many people on a Sunday afternoon driving alone. On Sunday afternoons in Britain many of us take a walk or even a drive, but we mostly do so with our families and friends. In California it seems many people, and most on the roads for walking is not the way they get around, are out on their own.

In his powerful vision of heaven and hell, *The Great Divorce*, C. S. Lewis portrays hell as a kind of grey and never-ending suburb where as you go further out the houses get further and further apart and all of them are single occupancy. Hell is the place where people who can't form relationships or stay in relationships end up living in lonely suburban individualism. Well the California suburbs are endless. I was living and working for a few months on the campus of Claremont Theological Seminary which is some forty miles west of downtown Los Angeles but still part of LA, and the suburban houses and commuters stretch on through Riverside to Palm Springs 50 miles away. But they are not grey. The sun does always seem to shine in California – though frequently obscured by smog – and the palm trees are everywhere just to prove it.

Individualism sure is pretty rife in that part of the world, and the built and the driven environment is physical testament to the mobility that promotes this individuality in this most postmodern and post-neighbourhood city. There are two six-lane and two 12-lane highways cutting through the 'community' of Claremont, giving the town a sense of transience, of not being a place unto itself, despite the intentions of those who planted a college-based New England style campus there called the Claremont Colleges, and built traditional clapboard homes, and planted trees around it.

Of course a lot of those folks on the freeway are probably driving to and from getting together with friends or family somewhere else. Or they are talking to friends on their cell phones as they drive – for it is still legal to do that in many American states. And that is another feature of life there. People are always on the move and their cars are like extensions of their houses, and often have phones and stereos and armchairs to match! People think nothing of driving 30 miles to church or commuting an hour and a half to work each way. And although the cars are mostly well equipped to keep the smog down, the large number of so-called Sports Utility Vehicles and pick-up trucks which are not regulated for emissions, means that smog is still a big problem after a week or so of sunshine.

The seminary where I was working is pretty liberal in its traditions and history and is also characterised by this fast-moving and individualistic lifestyle. Classes are organised on a timetable which allows each year of students to take all their courses in a two-day slot, enabling many students to commute in from Phoenix, San Diego and San Francisco. Many also live on site but the commuting timetable and the individualistic lifestyle makes for a residential community which still feels strangely disconnected. Despite its liberal heritage, the students cover the whole spectrum from evangelical and gospel churches to mainline Protestant, Methodist and Episcopal. And I found a warm welcome from the students for the way that I teach Christian ethics, and in particular my locating ethics within the scriptures and traditions of the Church, including worship and spirituality, instead of the more secular approaches to ethics you often find in liberal schools. I also found a great hunger to reconnect with the Christian tradition.

Christianity in the United States is so deeply divided and the liberal wing tends to distance itself from traditional Trinitarian and biblical doctrines and ethics, at least partly because so many of those who claim to speak from the tradition fail to critique the military imperialism and economic divides which the government and the media and the corporations, and especially the current President and administration, continue to ratchet up. There are progressive and environmentally aware evangelicals in the United States and their numbers are growing, while the liberal churches are in decline. But it is the car parks of the conservative churches here which tend to be fullest, and whose vehicles are most likely to sport the sad plastic American flags that 'patriots' have been adorning their cars, houses and clothing with since 9/11.

Witnessing to the Gospel, and living a Christian ethic, in that culture involves constant vigilance to the commercial and consumerist messages which plunder the airwaves, newspapers and skylines of that state and most others. The average American sees thousands of messages every week encouraging her to buy stuff and assuring her that buying stuff will save America from her enemies. The real truth – that the level of affluence in the United States (and yes, in Britain also) can only be sustained by unjustly oppressing workers and by destroying ecosystems in weaker and poorer countries, often identified as 'failed states' – is rarely aired, except it must be said on National Public Radio where, perhaps surprisingly, an alternative perspective is put across with greater vigour and radicalism, and with more information, than you would hear in any radio station in the UK.

Critics of the government in California are vocal and not cowed by the draconian legislation which Bush brought in after the events of September 11th, universally known as 9/11, which is also the telephone number you dial to call the emergency services Stateside. But the sad fact is that the United States is so vast, and its media so dominated by the quest for the corporate dollar, that most people just have no idea why 9/11 happened and nor do they really seem to want to know. This is especially so in California, perhaps partly because of location. By the time Californians get up in the morning, the rest of the world, barring Hawaii and Fiji, has already experienced and commented upon the significant events of the day!

In this culture the Gospel of Jesus Christ would be truly revolutionary. But in neither conservative nor liberal churches is the Gospel often presented in such a way as its revolutionary implications are heard. Virtually all of the messages – songs, preaching, prayers – that one hears in conservative churches are about individual needs and problems and plans and how God will meet these needs. There is no reference to the wider world of America, let alone of the environment, or the world beyond these wide shores. God is the fulfiller of individual aspirations to wealth and health, not the one who challenges us to risk all by living against the stream.

In liberal churches there is a good deal of reference to 'progressive' values such as justice, equality and peace, and prayers are said for peace in Palestine and Afghanistan, and for the wellness of creation. But loyalty and commitment to Christ as the one who can reshape our loves and our society is rarely preached alongside these progressive messages. You are more likely to hear how all people of whatever faith share in a common project to transform society. Interfaith dialogue does flourish here at local level – and not least since 9/11 when the mosques invited people of other faiths to worship with them and many did – and this is a great blessing. But it seems like the dialogue and healing that is needed just as much is between the liberal and conservative Christians, as the struggle for the soul of Christianity is in so many ways also a struggle for the soul of this powerful nation with its almost infinite capacity to visit good or evil on the larger world. And this is as true of the seminary where I was working – where all these issues are writ large amongst and between faculty and students – as it is for the churches.

'The preacher', the self-styled author of Ecclesiastes, speaks words of wisdom to the increasingly fractured and individuated nature of our postmodern world, and not least in that most postmodern of cities Los Angeles, which, through its movies, visits its values and vision of life so powerfully on the rest of us. Modern America, and increasingly modern Britain, are societies characterised by the condition of hypermobility in which machines, materials and men and women are constantly on the move. The noise of this movement is so invasive that it is rare to find a dwelling, or a moment in a day, when we do not hear the noise of a moving machine. And all this movement is strangely centripetal. It drives us apart from others. And it disconnects us from the material sources that constitute and construct the food and drink, clothing and materials on which we depend for our daily lives, in the home environment and in the workplace. We do not know who picked the coffee or the cotton we use everyday, who crafted the cheese we eat or the computer we use. We do not know what happened to the air or the animals, the water or the trees where these things were grown or made. And it is precisely because we do not know these things that the vigilance we might exercise if we did is absent. And because it is absent those who grow and make are often oppressed by the conditions in which they do these things.

At the beginning of the chapter from which my text is taken the preacher speaks of 'all the oppressions that are done under the sun' and of the 'tears of such as were oppressed' (4:1). Vanity for the preacher is 'evil work' (4:3). And evil work is work that oppresses, that is directed by those who have power against those who sew, and reap, in tears.

Many of the workers I met around the college and university site in Claremont were Mexicans. They could not afford to live in Claremont and often commuted up to two hours each way to reach the workplace. Many of those who labour in factories to make the clothes and computers sold in malls, in America and in Britain, are oppressed even more sorely; by inadequate reward, by intemperate bosses, and by miserable housing and diets. Hypermobility makes possible a degree of disconnectedness that not only promotes individualism but also oppression and irresponsibility in the making of the things that sustain our lives. And so from oppression and evil work we come to a situation where there is 'one alone, and not a second' and yet 'there is no end of all his labour'. Immoral making promotes both individualism and the idolatry of work without end.

In a world where neighbourhoods are increasingly fractured by hypermobility, it becomes harder to answer the question put to Jesus 'and who is my neighbour?' And yet Jesus responds not with a story about neighbourhoods but a story about mobility. The Samaritan, the true neighbour, meets the man who has fallen among thieves on the *road*. And so mobility is no excuse for irresponsibility but on the contrary, it is the *occasion* of connections of compassion and care.

The great twentieth-century theologian Karl Barth writes, in the third volume of his *Church Dogmatics*, about how the growing global connections that the modern machine world makes possible produce a situation in which we increasingly have both 'near and distant neighbours' within our sphere of responsibility.[24] And so our responsibility as Christians is to acknowledge and respond to the needs of those who are far off – and yet who give us those things that sustain our lives – as well as those who are near. And this is why at the back of church today you will find a

---

24 Karl Barth, *Church Dogmatics: The Doctrine of Creation*, trans. T. H. L. Parker et al., ed. G. W. Bromiley and T. F. Torrance, Vol. III.4 (Edinburgh: T & T Clark, 1961), 285.

stall on which you can buy a few of those things distantly grown and made, but marketed by Traidcraft as 'fairly traded' goods. Fair trade began as a project to do justice to distant neighbours, in India and Africa, who make and grow things we use in our daily lives, and who, under the rules of fair trade, are guaranteed a living wage, a reliable contract, and hence security that will enable them to escape the oppression of evil work. And in transacting with them to buy some of the things on which our disconnected lives depend we can begin to address the roots of a culture of bowling alone, of individualism, in which there is 'no end to labour.'

22. The Politics of Gentleness

November 2008

I will seek that which was lost, and bring again that which was driven away, and will bind up that which was broken, and will strengthen that which was sick: but I will destroy the fat and the strong; I will feed them with judgment.

Ezekiel 34:16

Inasmuch as you did it to one of the least of these, my brethren, you did it unto me.

Matthew 25:40

At great expense, and considerable inconvenience to bus drivers and other road users, the city council are redoing many junctions in Edinburgh at the moment, including the roads in Newhaven where I live. And what they are doing is putting in more metal barriers to segregate people from car drivers, keeping the pedestrians in virtual sheep pens while making the roads 'free' space for car drivers to drive up to, and often above, 30 miles per hour in built-up areas – or in other words at speeds that are dangerous to life and limb.

I am not good at being a sheep and since I don't currently own a car I resent the implication of these new road designs that provide freedom and space to car drivers who take precedence over pedestrians and cyclists. Human beings – pedestrians in particular – are not sheep. But all over Edinburgh, as the council continue to privilege the space for car mobility and car parking over pedestrians, the latter are restrained in overcrowded pavements that apparently the council never has any intention of widening no matter how crowded they get. At most times on South Bridge and South Clerk Street, as on parts of the Ferry

Road near where I live, there are more people on the pavements than in passing vehicles. But far more space is given to people in cars who are moving through the area than to pedestrians who live and shop and walk on the road.

Walking in Edinburgh is a dangerous activity, so dangerous that foreign students have to be warned not to step into the roads, even at junctions, because they are likely to be mown down. And indeed a number of foreign students are injured in such a way every year. Recently I had an experience that awakened me yet again to the dangers of walking in Edinburgh. I was walking – having broken my wrist – and not cycling to work through the New Town a few weeks ago and as I crossed an extensive but quiet cobbled junction a white van approached me in the middle of the crossing and hooted at me to indicate that I was in the way. Now the Highway Code clearly states that at uncontrolled junctions where pedestrians are already on the crossing they have a right of way over approaching vehicles. But how many drivers know this, or observe it? The result is that whenever one steps off the pavement at a junction without controlled lights and metal cages in Edinburgh one takes one's life in one's hands.

The preferential treatment by our city transport planners of motorised vehicles over pedestrians and cyclists is contrary to the officially declared UK government policy which promotes a hierarchy of users that suggests road and transport planners should design the streetscape so as to favour first the disabled, young children and pedestrians, then cyclists, then public transport, and lastly motorised private vehicles. But as with so much of central government policy this policy is more an aspiration – a centrally imposed target – than a reality in car-dominated Britain.

Many – and not least motorists – are opposed to this hierarchy and not least the drivers of private cars. Some, and it would seem this includes Edinburgh's own transport planners, have never heard of it. One influential city authority who knows about it and opposes it is the new Mayor of London, Boris Johnson. Though a cyclist himself he believes the hierarchy is wrong because it restricts the 'freedom' of road users, and in particular of private car drivers. But Boris like so many modern politicians does not know what true freedom is. I want to suggest that there are good moral, and even biblical, grounds for this governmental hierarchy of road users.

Listen to the words from our Old Testament reading this week:

> *I will seek that which was lost, and bring again that which was driven away, and will bind up that which was broken, and will strengthen that which was sick: but I will destroy the fat and the strong; I will feed them with judgment.*

Ezekiel 34:16

Ezekiel knows, as apparently Boris does not, that for the weak to have anything approaching equality and freedom the strong have to be restrained in their assertions of their own rights and freedoms.

In the Christian tradition this reverse hierarchy in which the weak are respected above the strong is supposed to be transposed into human hearts as our gospel this morning makes abundantly clear. The sheep, who are the righteous, are the gentle ones who attend to the weak, the stranger, the widow, the prisoner, the poor.

I heard last week in my own faculty of one such example of a retired colleague who used to visit inmates in Saughton prison when he was not entertaining students with his famous comparisons between Douglas Adams' *Hitchhiker's Guide to the Galaxy* and the New Testament. One individual whom he visited eventually got onto a day release programme and signed up for a Bachelor of Divinity degree in New College. And in this way my pipe-smoking, kilt-wearing, dog-loving aristocratic colleague of the old school was a real Christian. His compassion, gentleness and mercy led to the redeeming – if that is not too strong a claim to make for someone taking a BD at New College – of a prisoner.

Now I don't know if Boris Johnson would claim to be a real Christian but as a cyclist he should – but apparently does not – realise that for the roads to be safe places for people who are not surrounded by metal boxes and air bags those who are in the boxes need to be restrained from destroying the freedoms of the rest to move around, or even stand still.

The UK government in its latest road safety strategy consultation is asking for citizen views on a nationwide 20 mph limit in urban areas to reduce the death and serious injury toll on our roads. Why not write to your MP and say you approve, because it will prevent hundreds of serious injuries and deaths every year once signed into law?

An even more radical strategy for traffic management is under way in some towns and cities around Europe – though so far as I know none of these are in Scotland – including a few towns and villages in England and many more in the Netherlands, and Germany. And it is known as 'shared space'.

The concept of 'shared space' was first developed by Dutch traffic planner Hans Monderman who died this year. It involves removing all boundaries between different road users including kerbs and different levels of pavement and road, along with all traffic lights, pedestrian crossings, road paint and road signs. Instead all road users have to negotiate with each other for right of way. It has been found that this approach not only reduces accidents – to zero in many cases where it has been trialled – but also increases agency for all road users because it turns them all – drivers and walkers alike – into negotiators. It invites driver, cyclist and walker alike to be polite and, unlike the speed camera and the traffic light, it creates more considerate road users. Drivers respond by recovering moral agency, politeness, respect of those less strong than themselves and the whole urban environment is transformed. It is not as revolutionary as it might seem since many medieval towns – Siena for example – have such streetscapes still. But in the road-dominated urban areas where it is now being introduced it is a radical departure from conventional approaches to traffic management.

There is a deeper theological message here. We may read the parable of the sheep and goats as a parable of judgment that is above all about punishment and reward. Immanuel Kant and other enlightenment philosophers did not like the moral teachings of Jesus, or the Church, because they seemed to associate doing good with avoiding punishment. For Enlightenment philosophers like Scotland's David Hume, and Germany's Immanuel Kant, if people do the right thing only because they fear punishment, or are seeking the reward of a heavenly sheep field, this indicates they are not acting truly morally for it is only acts of goodness that are disinterested and freely chosen that can be said to be truly moral and truly free.

But this is entirely to misunderstand the teachings of Jesus and the moral import of the New Testament which is above all about love. And the meaning of love cannot be understood as an act conceived in isolation. Love is about connection, mutuality, relationship, shared well-being. The core message of the parable of the sheep and the goats is about recognition and discernment – the ones who have visited the sick and the prisoner, clothed the naked, fed the hungry did not do this as an act of religious zeal or under compulsion of any kind. They did it because they recognised in the other one who has an equal dignity to their own and responded to that. In so doing Jesus said they served him as well. Moral discernment is not about weighing a balance of consequences between road users or between rich and poor – no. The parable puts the emphasis on the weak. Those who side with the weak side with Christ who in his own ministry enacts an ethic of weakness, following what St Paul calls the kenosis of incarnation, and the royal road to the resurrection via the cross.

And so it is that when the early Christians come to reflect on the meaning of Christ's ministry, and the character of his kingly rule, they do not imagine him as an all-powerful king or a powerful heavenly judge but as a shepherd who came to seek and save the lost.

This is nowhere more evident than in early Christian art which again and again represents Christ as a good shepherd with a rescued lamb on his shoulders. There are no bloodied or tortured Christs in the first eight centuries of Christian art and for the first five there are no Christs sitting on imperial thrones or bedecked with crowns, sceptres or orbs. It is later in Byzantium that this becomes a standard way of depicting him.

The early Christian vision of rule is pastoral; it is one of rescue and remedy not of punishment and coercion. It issues in a politics of gentleness of the kind that puts the disabled pedestrian ahead of the car driver and invites the fastest driver to share space on an equal footing with the slowest pedestrian. The problem with the notions of freedom, and rule, that are operative in our society, and that Boris Johnson thinks he is upholding, is that the freedom of the strongest inevitably results in the oppression of the weakest.

Now I agree with Boris, and even Jeremy Clarkson, that coercion and punishment and speed cameras do not bring out the best in people, not even in car drivers. But it turns out that when enlightened traffic planners appeal to drivers' better natures they come through. When invited to drive as if *people* matter more than speed, drivers are capable of so doing. They respond intuitively to being invited, enabled – rather than coerced – into giving way to other, weaker, road users. This is the result of *pastoral* rule as opposed to the coercive rule of the CCTV camera, the pedestrian cage, the speed camera, and the traffic light.

23. Poverty, Empire and History

June 2005

Behold, your King comes to you: he is just, and having salvation; lowly, and riding upon an ass, and upon a colt the foal of an ass.

Zechariah 9:9

When President George W. Bush arrives in Scotland next week he will have an entourage which would make a Tudor monarch's court followers look insignificant. At the same time, off the West coast of Scotland there will be an aircraft carrier with a whole contingent of marines who have been given special permission to pursue any necessary military action inside Scotland under the direct command and control of the American military and outside the sovereign authority of Britain and its own defence and security apparatus. Not since William the Conqueror has Britain had on its soil a foreign potentate who claimed the right to exercise independent military force in these islands without recourse to the British head of state. This imperial presence, unprecedented in the last one thousand years of British history, unmasks the true nature of the assembly of world leaders known as the G8 in Gleneagles this week.

The nearest biblical equivalent to this extraordinary event is the arrival of the Queen of Sheba at the Court of King Solomon. Solomon you will remember had virtually enslaved the people of Israel in a deal with the family and household of King Hiram of Tyre to swap cedars from Lebanon with the forced labour of the Israelites. He then proceeded to build one of the grandest imperial projects of the ancient near east – Solomon's Temple – which was so gargantuan it would have absorbed about 400 St Jameses! The Queen of Sheba came to his court adorned with all the trappings of wealth to pay Solomon homage in recognition of his great economic and military prowess. She brought with her gifts to exchange – these included 120 talents of gold, large quantities of spices, and precious stones. So great were here gifts that never again, the writer of the book of the Kings tells us, were so many spices brought in as those the Queen of Sheba gave to King Solomon. And as we read on we discover that Solomon received so much gold from such gift exchanges and other trades that he was able to make shields for his army from it, to construct a grand throne of gold, and that all the eating utensils in his household were also of gold. He also accumulated horses and chariots in their hundreds.

Solomon is described as wealthier and more powerful than any other of the kings of Israel. But the books of Kings in which his great wealth is described is ultimately a history of the corruption, division and exile of the Houses of Israel and Judah. The Kings of Israel, the writers tell us, were corrupted by their great power and wealth and they neglected the covenant that their forefathers had made with the God of Moses, to keep his commandments forever. And was it not Solomon who had his subjects labour on foreign hills to log cedars for his temple, and in mines digging for gold?

The story of the imperial trading economy advanced by the World Trade Organization and the corporations and wealthy nations of the earth – whose leaders meet in Gleneagles this week – is presaged in the books of Samuel and Kings. When the people of Israel first asked God for a king the prophet Samuel told them that it was a bad idea, and they were better off as a confederation ruled by the seventy judges. And God told Samuel to tell them that if they did get a king, he would enslave them and their children to his foreign wars and imperial projects and eventually they would come crying to God to deliver them and God would be unable so to do.

If God could not deliver the Israelites from their corrupt kings, but consigned them instead to exile from the Promised Land in punishment for their corrupt imperial designs, then what might we expect God to do for the peoples of Africa, South Asia,

Central and South America who labour today under a burden of poverty so great that a child dies every three seconds?

But today's Old Testament reading in a sense already contains the answer that God gives to the people whom their corrupt leaders had consigned to exile:

> *Rejoice greatly, O daughter of Zion; shout, O daughter of Jerusalem: behold, your King comes to you: he is just, and having salvation; lowly, and riding upon an ass, and upon a colt the foal of an ass. And I will cut off the chariot from Ephraim, and the horse from Jerusalem, and the battle bow shall be cut off: and he shall speak peace unto the heathen: and his dominion shall be from sea even to sea, and from the river even to the ends of the earth.*

Zechariah 9:9–10

We know to whom this reading refers for was it not just eight weeks ago that we walked around our churches waving our palm branches and shouting 'Hosanna to the Son of David, Blessed is he who comes in the name of the Lord.' Christ came – he was a king and yet he rode on a donkey, with a colt beside him, and spurned war horses and chariots. He commanded peace to the nations, and ever since his Ascension as Risen Lord Christians have proclaimed his dominion from sea to shining sea.

But what does this dominion mean when the born-again Christian President of the most powerful empire the world has ever known commands a military machine which has 800 bases spread around every continent, and negotiates trade deals which favour his country's corporations and their ability to extract cheap labour and natural resources at knock-down prices from every country on earth to sustain the great Wal-mart-led economy which is modern America?

With Tony Blair and Gordon Brown effectively claiming the Make Poverty History march this weekend as part of their New Labour project it would seem that the main aim of the Make Poverty History march in Edinburgh is to persuade President George W. Bush, and the United States, to move from a self-interested imperial stance towards the poor nations in the South to one of shared intent to abolish poverty by abolishing debt, changing the unfair rules of global trade and giving them more aid. And have we not already had some success according to Mr Blair and Mr Brown because an agreement has already been made to cancel the outstanding debts of the world's poorest countries?

At this point I begin to suspect that we are deceived. Look at the small print of the debt deal and look at what Mr Blair and Mr Brown's government are actually doing in their trade and aid with small impoverished countries in the South. Under the Heavily Indebted Poor Countries programme conditionalities are imposed on countries such as Uganda and Tanzania which require their governments to stop protecting small farmers from international competition, to allow foreign corporations to fish in their waters, log their forests and grow food on their lands, to privatise public services, and to devalue their currencies. HIPC has provided rich pickings for European and American corporations who have bought up the land, labour, resources and public services of these impoverished nations at knock-down prices.

Christians have campaigned for Third World debt relief since the 1980s, and the recent Jubilee campaign did in some measure provoke a significant write-off of debt in the last few years. But nonetheless the conditions imposed have seriously dented the value – both moral and fiscal – of the write-offs. And they are a tragic indication of the continuing willingness of wealthy developed countries to extract tribute from the poorest and most indebted peoples on earth. In this context the slogan of the present campaign – Make Poverty History – looks hubristic as well as unrealistic.

When Jesus rode into Jerusalem on the donkey his procession not only recalled the prophetic words of Zechariah. It also affirmed that the rule of the Prince of Peace was unlike the rule of earthly princes and emperors. Jerusalem was the headquarters of Roman rule over Palestine in his day and the temple, whose precincts he was soon to visit, was the headquarters of the tax gatherers who received and passed on tribute to Caesar. And hence the form of his visit to the great city was both one of humility and of judgment. Having ridden on a foal of a donkey the next day he takes up a whip to drive out the moneychangers from the temple precincts.

Through the centuries Christians came to worship Christ as Pantocrator – the one who rules over the earth from heaven. But in so doing they celebrate a different kind of rule than the traditional dominion of men. In this new dominion every individual has a relationship directly to the heavenly ruler since the rule of the Pantocrator is written on the human heart. And the nature of this rule produced something new in world history that had rarely been seen before and this was a civilisation of free cities and craftsmen, self-sufficient farmers and fisherfolk, peasants and nobles. Through the history of Christendom slavery and feu or debt-bondage – of the kind that had been customary in previous civilisations including the Egyptian, the Babylonian, the Persian, the Chinese and the Roman – gradually dissolved. This dissolution took place in what modern historians have trained us to call the 'dark ages'. But in fact, as the American sociologist Rodney Stark argues in his recent book *The Victory of Reason*, there took place in the Middle Ages a significant cultural shift because of the influence of Catholic Christianity throughout Europe, and the Church's teaching about the value of the individual before God, and hence of the needful restraints on the power of princes and the wealthy. This teaching and its influence led to the gradual freeing of serfs and slaves from coercive conditionalities and a growing spread of property and freedom in the countries of Christendom so that by the time of the Reformation peasants largely lived free in rural Britain, as did the craftsmen and merchants in the towns. And this principle of freedom produced a desire for freedom from external tutelage over Britain, whether from the monarchic and princely power of the popes in Rome, or from wealthy and corrupt prince bishops and cardinals at home.

But just as people were being released from coerced servitude at home so in the colonies the princes of Europe reinvented slavery, first in the Canary Islands, then in South America, and subsequently in the East and West Indies, and the New World. Despite papal bulls, and puritan protests, against these developments the Church is now blamed for this history of slavery and its noble history as the root of freedom and democracy in European Christendom is now forgotten or denied.

And so it is this weekend. The slogan 'Make Poverty History' implies that history is the dustbin of the past into which coercive poverty can be consigned. In reality the progress of the modern industrial world from the Christian Middle Ages to the secular industrial present has been one of the gradual spread of the coercion of wage labour, and its alternative of enforced idleness or unemployment, both of them occasioned by the gradual loss of property and self-sufficiency among the great mass of humanity, first in the First World and now in the Third.

Last week I met a taxi driver in Nottingham. He was from Peshawar and described his job as one of slavery. He had to work 12 hours a day to feed, clothe and house his family and provide a college education for his daughters. It is hard to defend the progress of the Christian West to such a man when in his home city militarist and economic incursions from the West continue to occasion the loss of the traditional self-sufficiency of the people of Pakistan and drive many, deprived of their secure livelihood, to seek wage labour elsewhere. Pakistan is a country where the majority still live on less than two dollars a day, and where many do not receive even a primary education. But as subsidised foods and manufactures arrive on their doorstep their traditional non-cash and self-sufficient economy is gradually dissolving, and poverty and strife grow apace.

Imperial trade and the wars that accompany it have been the driving force of dissolution and exile from the time of the Kings of Israel to the era of the G8. Against an imperial economy based on a war footing Jesus rides into Jerusalem on a foal. His rule is a gentle rule and it promises liberation to the poor, not through military prowess, but through recognition of their right to justice and self-sufficiency, and through redemption from debt. In Israel in Jesus' day the peasants were losing their land because of debts occasioned by the taxes of the Roman imperium. In China and

Industan today peasants lose their lands to a similar, though even more global, imperium. Redemption from debt, and from the coercion of poverty wages, is still the cry of the poor. But we should not fool ourselves that the powerful will give them back the lands the global economy is stealing from them.

I wonder then, when Blair and Brown give the visiting leaders a short *tour d'horizon* of the nation of Scotland in which they gather at Gleneagles, if reference will be made to the Scottish Parliament's Land Reform Act. I suspect not, somehow, for at the heart of this act is the biblical principle, emanating from the Prophets and Torah, that tenants who dwell under the coercive rule of powerful lairds or princes are not free. And their unfreedom is an offence against divine justice, and against the biblical claim, enshrined in old Scots law, that the earth belongs to the Lord and not to the Laird, and that the rule of the Lord is a gentle rule wherein their is no coercion, no debt bondage, no involuntary poverty.

24. Calvin, Benedict and the Credit Crunch

October 2008

You cannot serve God and mammon.

Matthew 6:24

The Bank of Scotland is one of the world's oldest banks and the first private bank to issue paper money. It was inaugurated a few hundred yards from this church by the merchants of Edinburgh who had heard from John Knox, who learned it from Jean Calvin in Geneva, that lending money at interest was no longer a sin against God. The Bank's collapse a few weeks ago was because it was laden with debt, in part because of its merger with the Halifax, which was Britain's largest demutualised building society. A mutual is essentially a cooperative: it is owned by its savers and can lend as much as it has in its savings accounts. And this was how the Bank of Scotland itself originally worked. A mutual society is locally owned by its lenders and borrowers and it has a debt ratio of one to one – what it takes in in the form of cash it can lend out, and no more! Its shares are in the form of savings and so cannot be traded in anonymous deals on the stock market and sold short in the complex chicaneries of the hedge funds' and other stock markets' devices for gambling released on the world by the 1987 Big Bang. These weird devices for making money out of money were invented by university-trained economists, enabled in this by government lawmakers who deregulated money on their advice. And as a result in this country, and in the United States, for the last thirty years money has been the master. As Jesus said – and as we now see in the financial meltdown since Lehmann Brothers collapsed, and its tragic effects in the lives of millions of ordinary people who are losing their jobs and homes, and millions of others going hungry because of the high price of food – you cannot serve God and money. Money is not just a poor sovereign. As a sovereign it replaces God, and undermines the laws of God; it multiplies debt and bondage; and it destroys communities, families, homes, livelihoods and ultimately the earth itself.

For hairy lefties like me – and we are an endangered species – the last few days have provided a bit of satisfaction, a feeling of 'I told you so'. Money is a tyrannical sovereign. When money and its agents are freed from legal restraint then people and the earth are enslaved and vice grows while godliness and contentment – to use St Paul's language in his letter to Timothy – decline. The moral decline of Britain and America in the last thirty years reached its nadir in the events of the war on terror when just war precepts that had restrained torture were torn up as our leaders went over to what Vice-President Dick Cheney called the 'dark side'. And this nadir is equally evident in the terrible inequality that the monetary libertarians have loosed on our two nations. Inequality fuels violence and violence grows in our streets, as well as in our foreign policy. But our leaders are determined that money will continue to rule, rescued by the state on yet more unwise borrowings against the future.

But is man any better than money as a sovereign? Two weeks ago I was getting a cricked neck looking up at Michelangelo's famous depiction, in the Sistine Chapel, of God creating Adam and Eve in Rome. Man being made, fashioned, shaped in the image of God is nowhere more memorably depicted than in this great painting. But is the proud and graceful image of the heavily muscled Michelangelo Adam what Hebrew theologians had in mind when they penned the Genesis account of the origins of humanity? The Renaissance dethroned God and enthroned man as 'the measure of all things', recasting a doctrine of ancient Greece in stone and bronze, and in the assertion of human sovereignty in the nation states that have risen in Europe in the last four hundred years and colonised much of the planet. Adam in the Sistine Chapel is Renaissance man – this is no humble tiller of the soil.

Adam means son of the soil – Adam is of the earth and his first work is to till the earth and to draw out its potential. And in the Museum of Early Christian Art which I also visited in the Vatican there are some wonderful sarcophagi from the second and third centuries on one of which is depicted a much more modest image of Adam and Eve on the verge of being evicted from the garden. God gives them a spiked staff to till the earth. In this image humans are partners with God's creation – they are not lords of it, nor sovereigns. In Hebrew the word dominion is *radah*, and it is better interpreted as vice-regency than sovereignty or dominion. But after the Fall there is only a flawed representation of divinity on earth, until that is Christ comes to heal and restore the image of God in humanity. And even Christ eschews imperial rule and sovereign power. The early Christians understood this when they depicted Christ as the good shepherd, not as a heavenly king. And as a shepherd, and not Caesar, early Christian art depicts rule very differently from the Roman. Whereas Rome gloried in imperious power, and imaged it in violent combat, hunting and war, in early Christian art there are no images of hunting or predation; no celebration of blood or gore. Even the cross itself – that cruel bloody instrument of imperial torture – is depicted peaceably, as a tree under which are depicted, on a number of sarcophagi, shepherds and sheep sheltering under its branches.

Early Christian art recalls the idealised world of Eden in which also there was according to the story no killing. Not only are Adam and Eve, in Genesis 1—3, instructed to be vegetarians. Even the wild animals are told to eat grasses and fruits and not each other. Of course this is an idealised image. But it serves a theological purpose. Agriculture is read by the Hebrew editors of the text as indicative of humanity's fallen dominion over the earth. And the move to agriculture, from the gathering of fruits that humanity had earlier practised, came at a great price as we learn in the fourth chapter of Genesis, when Cain kills Abel with an agricultural implement. Looking back on their terrible history of violence the Hebrew theologians imagine a time in Genesis 1 and 2 when there was no violence, no killing, but instead original blessing, primeval peace. The story of evolution would indicate there was never such a time. But the creation story indicates that though there is violence, before violence there is peace. And Christ comes to restore peace on earth by his non-violent witness to a different kind of sovereignty. The Good Shepherd is not the Magisterium, nor a dweller in palaces and marbled halls. His is a gentle pastoral rule and he promises that when we so model our relations with one another we will find peace on earth and with the other creatures.

What does this look like in practice? For me it is another Benedict than the one I saw enthroned in a *Star Trek*-style audience room in the Vatican two weeks ago who shows the way. After Rome and Christianity came together in an ambiguous alliance in the fourth century the Christian world changed. Some, like the Mennonite theologian John Howard Yoder in his *Politics of Jesus*, see this as the second fall, the fall of Christianity that mirrored the fall of Adam and Eve in Eden. As the corruption of Rome near its end – with all its licentiousness and violence – seeped into the pores of the Church, there were those Christian brothers and sisters who felt they had to leave the compromises of imperial Rome behind and they took to the desert. Initially they were hermits and lived off the gifts of those who came to take their counsel. But in time the hermits formed communities and these communities formed in Benedict's great rule an order of life which recalled in many ways the mythic world of the Garden of Eden.

The Romans believed manual labour was only fit for peasants and slaves. But in Benedict's rule Adam's call to till the soil is redeemed and a new way of life becomes thinkable in which soul and soil are both restored in the balanced life of work and worship, earthkeeping and contemplative study and prayer. Ultimately the monks became so successful at farming that their wealth spoiled them. Some might say the beer and wine also addled their brains, as many a bottle of Benedictine 'Bucky' does the brains of those who still live on Edinburgh's streets. But the spirit of Benedict lives on, and is even being revived in a renewal of interest in the contemplative life around the world. And alongside that renewal there is another revival which is equally Benedictine in spirit and this is the revival of interest in real food, and in the desire to grow it as well as eat it.

My family have recently acquired the shared use of half an acre of land and over the summer I began the hard work of digging out the weeds from some of its undug beds while also enjoying the fruits of another's labours on other vegetable and fruit beds. Despite my admiration for Benedict in theory I have still been surprised in practice to discover just how sensually and spiritually satisfying digging the ground is. Yes I have been pulling out brambles and nettles and stones by the barrow load, but in it I have felt fulfilled, enriched, embodied, in a way I have not for years. To my surprise there is something rather sensual about digging, planting and weeding whose end is the growing food – and not just exterior design. It produces a sustaining and lasting satisfaction.

A couple of months ago I visited an allotment close to Cameron Toll which was established by the city of Edinburgh for people with psychological problems of various kinds. The young community worker who showed us round was inspiring and told us how many of those who were referred to her by GPs and psychiatrists had never dug before, or successfully grown and nurtured anything in their lives. But for most of them the experience of planting, tending, and harvesting vegetables had been deeply therapeutic. And she told of people who had been freed from addictions of various kinds, who had found healing from abusive or failed relationships with partners or children, and who had recovered dignity and purpose in lives in which these had been mind-alteringly lacking.

The monks became very good at digging, planting and harvesting, so good in fact that their monasteries grew wealthy. And so it was that they began to keep books and ledgers to account for their wealth, and invented double-entry book-keeping. And was it not failings in accounting which led to the collapse of Edinburgh's great banks, including the Bank of Scotland? Ultimately the monks were corrupted by their wealth so that many of them grew fat and ceased from manual labour. And as Dom Sorge argues in his little book *Holy Work*, in the demise of Benedict's rule of the holy life – in which manual, intellectual and spiritual work are held in balance – were the seeds of the corruption and downfall of monasticism.

In Edinburgh today, and in every financial centre, a related corruption and downfall is upon us. We now know that the banks had ways of keeping things off the ledger, that they invented new kinds of ledger far beyond the imaginings of monkish accounting, and that sometimes they did not properly examine the ledger before taking on significant – and in the case of RBS, bank-destroying – risks. Monetary accounting has become as open to corruption as any other of the practices inherited from Christendom. And Christians have been in the vanguard of those who are pushing for new kinds of accounting – social accounting, ecological accounting, ethical accounting – so that the hidden costs, and potential corruption, of monetary transactions can be made known.

One way local churches are doing this in Britain is through the Ecocongregation network. The Ecocongregation approach to church organisation encourages a different kind of accounting to one solely focused on money, and which draws on the practice of ecological footprinting invented by a professor of ecology in Vancouver some years ago. In becoming an ecocongregation, the local church looks not only at the monetary balance sheet but at other measures of activity such as the greenhouse gases emitted by buildings and modes of travel to church, the sustainability of the foods, fuels and fibres used around the church, and the wastes disposed of or recycled. Ecocongregationalism is a way of bringing the fullness of the Benedictine rule into the life of the church community. And like that rule its impacts and meanings are not confined to the balance sheets or even to greenhouse gas accounts. A flourishing ecocongregation finds a growing range of ways of reconnecting the life and worship of the church, and the daily lives of its members, with the healing and restoring of God's good earth.

The practices encouraged by the ecocongregation movement involve resistance to the sovereignty of money by the local church, and a recovery of true representative rule: rule as care for God's creation; as attention to the needs of all God's creatures; and as responsibility in material and social relations. This is a humbler vision of human sovereignty than that dreamed of in Charlotte Square or the Bank on the Mound, and one which the shepherd of our souls would surely recognise as a seed of the kingdom.

25. Trust and Obey

October 1999

I am the good shepherd.

John 10:11

A few weeks ago a friend of mine was being wheeled into the operating theatre prior to a rather invasive surgical procedure at the Western General Hospital when he was told by the consultant surgeon that a consequence of the procedure would be that a crucial part of his digestive and eliminatory system would not work normally anymore. At this point he sat up on the bed and said that he no longer wished to proceed with the operation. The consultant was very angry and declared that he was sure my friend had already been told the information by one of his junior doctors and that he was unwise to pull out of the operation now. My friend insisted that he had not consented to the procedure on the basis of full information and no longer wanted to go through with it. And after signing the usual disclaimer, he called a taxi and went home. He got better eventually without surgical intervention and has never once doubted that he took the right decision.

Trust is a funny thing. On the one hand a lot of aspects of human life and social experience would be pretty problematic without it. We would be hard put to pay our bills if we did not trust our bank to honour our cheques or organise payment of direct debits or standing orders. We might never go on a journey if we did not place a considerable degree of trust in train drivers or pilots, air traffic controllers and maintenance engineers.

But on the other hand we often hear it said of someone in a particular situation – perhaps they bought a dodgy second-hand car or took on a badly performing endowment mortgage – that they were too trusting of salesmen or lawyers. We need to display trust in our relations with others for without it we will lead anxious lives and be prone to control freakery. Deeply distrustful managers are difficult to work for because they won't delegate and when they do they won't trust those delegated to do the work well. Distrustful people are rather good at establishing conditions in which things do actually often turn out badly because in a sense they create the conditions for others to behave badly – incapable of trust they produce suspicion and anxiety and make it hard for others to perform well.

Sheep are on the whole pretty trusting animals for they lack the brain power to be critical or suspicious either of one another or of other agents in whose charge they may be, sheep dogs and shepherds for example, or more often the ram who just happens to be in the front today, leading the rest of the flock goodness knows where. And yet sheep are the animal of choice when it comes to the analogies that the Gospel of John gives us for the kinds of trust Christians are to display in their relations with their Lord. Talking to the Jews who don't trust his claims about himself, Jesus declares this is because 'you do not belong to my sheep. My sheep hear my voice; I know them and they follow me' (John 10:27). Similarly in the Gospel of Matthew, Jesus sends out the disciples on a mission as 'sheep in the midst of wolves' (Matt. 10:16), and in the parable of the sheep and the goats it is sheep who do the will of God – visiting the sick and the prisoners and feeding the hungry – while goats, as anyone who has spent any time with them knows, tend to be more cussed and independent minded, are those who neglect to do the will of God.

This leaves us moderns with a bit of a problem, and it is not simply that since we are no longer a pastoral society we don't know much about the character of either sheep or goats and hence they are pretty poor analogies for us. No; it is rather that we live in a society whose ideal of the human person is not of sheep but rather of goats. We are exhorted in news stories, novels and biographies to admire those people who are independent minded and who can get along pretty much on their own resources or as heroic leaders of others who follow in their impressive individualistic wake – Shackleton the explorer,

Churchill the lone political opponent of Hitler, Diana the independent-minded princess of hearts.

Hero-worship has an ancient history as witness the classical stories of Odysseus or Perseus on which I was raised. But the modern adulation of the individual reflects a more recent narration of the individual in charge of her own life, freed from the tutelage of God, Church, Scripture, and tradition. The philosophers of the Enlightenment and the modern age constructed an ideal of autonomy, of sovereign individual rights, whose legacy we are still discovering. One consequence is that people feel their only public duty is to follow their own interests as far as possible, limited only by the rule that we do not unfairly limit others' freedom. As my friend Stanley Hauerwas puts it, 'As a result we have found it increasingly necessary to substitute procedures and competition for the absence of public virtues. The bureaucracies in our lives are not simply the result of the complexities of an industrialized society, but a requirement of a social order individualistically organized.'[25]

One of the outcomes is a diminishment in trust and mutual aid, and its substitution with supposedly objective mechanisms of accountability and control, and especially those of the accountant and the management consultant. As a consequence we are living in what one writer describes as the 'audit society'. Such a society imposes audits and targets on institutions and professions as 'rituals of verification' designed to ensure that people are doing what they say they are, and that what they are doing can be measured by the accountant's rule. Many of the professions – medicine, law, teaching – on which these rituals are now visited had their roots in Christian beliefs and practices.

As Christians we are not called blindly to follow the traditions of any profession, any more than to heedlessly submit to the 'quality audits' imposed by bureaucrats. But it might be good to remind ourselves that the ideals of the professional, the reason why we mostly still find them trustworthy, find their origin not in audit but in a tradition which placed enormous emphasis on

---

25 Stanley Hauerwas and Charles Pinches, *Christians Among the Virtues: Theological Conversations with Ancient and Modern Ethics* (Notre Dame, IN: University of Notre Dame Press, 1999), 127.

the importance of following the Master who himself healed the sick, revealed the new law of love, and taught the multitude the wisdom of his teaching as one with authority.

It is this authority which confers trustworthiness on the life Jesus lived, and the teachings and ordinances he left behind. For it is from God, as the Gospel of John in particular frequently reminds us, that Jesus derives his authority. His teachings are valid because he received them from God and from no other source.

God is the maker. He knows our good because he created us. He designed the creature and now in Jesus he restores it to its full potential. Trust in what life throws at us is sometimes incredibly hard. It is OK when things are going well to trust that God our maker is also our provider and our redeemer. It is a great deal harder to believe in providence when things are going badly. The temptation is to try to control events to reduce the risk that they do. And yet the whole point of the sheep analogy is that as Christians we are called to live life 'out of control'. As Stanley Hauerwas, puts it: 'To live out of control as Christians means that we do not assume that our task as Christians is to make history come out right ... those who are without control have fewer illusions about what makes this world secure or safe: and they inherently distrust those who say they are going to help through power or violence.'[26]

As Christians we trust in God because all that God tells us about God's self and all that God has done for us in Jesus Christ reveals that God is trustworthy. Yes there are times when it seems that independent, autonomous, self-willing individuals are truly fulfilled and it is we Christians – the sheep – who suffer unjustly. But it is precisely at such times we all the more need to adopt the attitude of sheep to their shepherd – to trust that God is in this set of events, this chain of circumstances, that God is able to sustain us through it.

There are three things that we can do to make things come out better in a society lacking in trust. The first is to raise children who learn the value of trust – trust in the love and care of their

---

26 Stanley Hauerwas, 'The Servant Community: Christian Social Ethics' in *The Hauerwas Reader*, ed. John Berkman and Michael Cartwright (Durham, NC: Duke University Press, 2001), 381.

maker and trust in the love and care of their parents. Trusting people are people who have had from their earliest years experiences of dependable parenting; and the control freaks around us are often those who have not.

The second is to develop our own rituals of verification, to remind ourselves every day that God made us, that he loves and sustains us, and that he calls us to be sheep in a world of goats. We are invited to trust God and it is that trust which enables us to trust one another. Reading the Bible, meditating on scenes from the life of Christ, and interceding for the world – these are the things which, as sheep, we have to do daily if we are not to be tempted to become like the goats and imagine we can do today alone, without reference to the shepherd.

The third is to trust in surprises. Christians are people who enjoy surprises and are able to welcome them into their lives. And the outcome of such trust is joy for again, as Hauerwas puts it: 'Joy is the result of letting go of the slim reed of security that we think provides us with the power to control our own and others' lives ... Joy is thus finally a result of our being dispossessed of the illusion of security and power that is the breeding ground of our violence.'[27]

---

27   Hauerwas, *Peaceable Kingdom*, 148.

26. Global Scattering and Christian Communion

But this people have a rebellious heart; they have revolted and gone.
Neither say they in their heart, Let us now fear the LORD our God, that
giveth rain, both the former and the latter, in his season: he reserveth unto
us the appointed weeks of the harvest. Your iniquities have turned away
these things, and your sins have withholden good things from you.

Jeremiah 6:23–25

Remember that you were once without Christ, once aliens from the
commonwealth of Israel, strangers to the covenant of promise, having no
hope, without God in the world. But now in Christ Jesus you who once
were far off have been brought near by the blood of Christ.

Ephesians 2:14, 15

Less than two years ago the land of Britain was devastated by the
unnecessary slaughter of millions of animals. Smoke from the
funeral pyres which were unwisely lit to destroy them could be
smelt in Holland. I say unwisely because the Chief Veterinary
Officer had recommended that the government vaccinate the
national herd – as many other countries do – instead of slaughtering millions of cows. But after a conference was called of
farmers, veterinarians and agriculture officials to discuss the
implementation of this policy, the chief executive of Nestlé, a
company which has a large powdered milk factory in Cumbria,
protested to the Prime Minister that if the UK vaccinated the
export of powdered milk to the developing world would be
compromised. And to save the profits of this dubious enterprise –
dubious because the milk is often promoted as being superior to
breast milk in places where mothers do not have access to clean
water or sterilisation equipment – the government eventually

decided to go ahead with the slaughter. And still there are rotting piles of carcasses inadequately treated and buried in the soil which are even now polluting water courses in some parts of North Briton, including Cumbria, Northumberland and Lanarkshire.

Some said that this plague, and the burning and destruction which followed, are a judgment on modern agriculture, and in particular on modern methods of animal husbandry. But only twelve months after Britain was declared foot-and-mouth free, the hills of England, Wales and Scotland are once again full to overflowing with the gambolling and bleating of lambs, and the milk parlours and pastures full of mooing of cows. The government in its unwisdom, instead of taking this opportunity to refashion the farming industry and move it towards a more sustainable, and kinder, approach to animal husbandry, offered blanket compensation to every farmer and with this vast subsidy to an already problematic and bloated animal industry the numbers of sheep and cattle in Britain now exceed the numbers before the outbreak of foot-and-mouth.

Rearing animals for meat and milk protein for human consumption is an age-old practice. The Israelites were first nomadic tribesmen who followed their flocks to pasture in the fertile lands of Mesopotamia between the Tigris and the Euphrates – land that is modern-day Iraq – and wound up in Egypt when a particularly harsh drought left the Nile valley with the only good pasturage in the ancient Near East. They later were liberated from the Pharaohs in a nation-forming saga and eventually moved to the lands contiguous with modern-day Palestine/ Israel. By the time of Jeremiah they no longer lived in tents among their sheep but in large cities which were capable of making war on their neighbours. These cities were places of great temptation for the Israelites who gradually abandoned the commandments and rituals which Yahweh had given to their ancestor sheep farmers and goat herdsmen at Sinai in the wilderness.

So sophisticated did the urban Israelites become that some lived in fine houses with many servants and governed great estates with hundreds of sheep and cows, vines and olive trees, and fields of wheat and corn. Israel became so rich and powerful that it began to behave like an empire, conquering and annexing land for hundreds of miles around. But at the same time many of the Israelites themselves were reduced to the status of wage slave, serving the large estates or the empire of Israel with no fig tree or vineyard of their own with which to feed their children. Having once abandoned the communal and simpler society of their ancestors it was only natural that the Israelites would also abandon the worship of Yahweh for the cults of the Egyptians and the Philistines, the Babylonians and Assyrians. These cults represented in gods of gold and diamond, precious stone and carved rock, a hierarchy of heavenly beings which symbolised in the heavenly pantheon the social hierarchy of rich and powerful, weak and enslaved, and even the necessity of human sacrifice. The new gods then more satisfactorily mirrored the social structure of the new urban Israel.

According to the prophets of ancient Israel from Isaiah and Jeremiah to Amos and Micah the Israelites were scattered like sheep without a shepherd because of the judgment of God. Their exile was not just a consequence of the military and political superiority of the kings and nations who conquered them. Rather their exile in the kingdoms of Persia, Babylon and Assyria was the judgment of God for their abandonment of the ways of God – their failure to worship the one God of Abraham and Isaac and Jacob, their worship of idols instead, and their failure to keep the laws of this one God as revealed to Moses. Their exile was also a consequence of their abuse of the land. They so overburdened the land with their animals and the demands of their growing armies for bread and meat that the land was turning to desert, losing its fertility, so that one acre of wheat would give only one bushel where once it had given ten, and even their vineyards failed. Nature, as well as God, turned against them because they had abandoned the laws of God, and by abandoning God's justice they had neglected also the justice not only of human society but of the land itself.

The scattering of Israel then was a political, an ecological and an economic event. So for example archaeologists have found evidence that the once great city of Jericho was rapidly abandoned some time around the eighth or seventh century BCE because the land around it had become so dry, its soil so depleted, that it could no longer support the inhabitants of so great a city.

Whatever the state of British farming we would not seem to have come to such a pass, or even to be at risk of so doing. But the story of British agriculture is somewhat more complex than that of Israelite agriculture. I read in the *Independent* while on holiday in France that the Amazonian rainforest – the last truly great area of tropical forest remaining on earth – was destroyed at a faster rate in the last five years than ever before. An area the size of England has disappeared every year for the last five years. At this rate of destruction no old growth tropical rainforest will remain in twenty years. And what is the cause of this destruction? One of the main ones is the European and American demand for animal feed. All these animals which we keep in the often cold and damp pastures of Britain require a lot of feeding. They cannot get by on grass alone, and especially not in the long winters. In Scotland so cold is the climate that cattle in particular are fed cattle cake in sheds for up to eight months of the year, and pigs likewise are reared more indoors than out. Even sheep need supplemental feeding for six months in the year. One of the principal uses to which cleared land in the Amazon is being put is the growing of soya to meet the ever-growing European and American demand for animal feed. This demand is so great that it distorts world food markets and world agriculture to such an extent that in many developing countries more land is given over to the growing of crops for consumption by foreign animals than for consumption by local humans.

All of this would be bad enough but it is made ten times worse by the European Common Agricultural Policy. The size of production subsidies to European farmers to produce food no one wants remains at over 40 billion Euros, or half the total budget of the European Union. This vast subsidy not only leads to over-production and over-consumption of precious resources, including Amazonian rain forest land for soya production. It also leads to this excess food being dumped on food markets in the developing world, so devastating farmer incomes in developing countries, and ultimately contributing to poverty and famine in many countries in the South.

At the same time as Europe is dumping this vast quantity of subsidised food in the South and destroying agricultural markets outside its borders, Europe is also erecting a ring of steel and computers around its borders. We may export food and destroy small farmers in the South, but we won't allow those whose lives and lands our policies destroy to come and live in Europe. We feed each one of our cattle here in Scotland more protein than millions of families in the South look forward to in their daily diets. But when people from the South attempt to come and live among us we let them drown in boats in the Mediterranean, we tell them they are not welcome, and if they make it through Europe's immigration defences we put them in miserable tower blocks and give them food vouchers, so they are marked out as strangers and aliens.

If there is one thing that living in a global economy means it is that people are exiled from their land; the sheep are well and truly scattered. Because of the 'free trade' policies enforced on indebted countries by the World Bank and the International Monetary Fund, and backed up by the World Trade Organization, weak developing countries are allowed no protection from the devastating effects of foreign economic power in the form of subsidised cheap foods or predatory transnational corporations cherry picking resources in the South – whether oil and diamonds, or public water supplies and telephone networks. And so small farmers lose their lands, tribal peoples are burned out of their forests, fisherfolk lose access to the coastal waters fished by their ancestors, and even townspeople find their savings turned to nothing – as have the people of Argentina or more recently Iraq – as the great warlike machine of the global economy consumes all before it.

> 'Remember that you were once without Christ' says St Paul to the Ephesians, 'once aliens from the commonwealth of Israel' 'strangers to the covenant of promise' 'having no hope, without

God in the world. But now in Christ Jesus you who once were far off have been brought near by the blood of Christ.

Ephesians 2:14,15

In the context of all I have been saying these words have a greater power than they could have to us merely as citizens of Britain and the European Union. We are in truth inheritors of the promise, the promise of the global economy – we dwell in prosperity, if not always in peace. Our bellies are full, our houses replete with things made by labourers in other lands. It is as if the promises to Israel after exile – that nations would come and serve her once she is reinstalled in the land of promise – have already come true through the power of our governments, corporations and the collective power of the European Union. How could we know what it is to be exiled, to be excluded from the commonwealth? We live inside the fence, and only occasionally glimpse what it means to live outside when we see a headline about an over-crowded boat of refugees going down in the Mediterranean, or a lorry with a hidden cargo of human beings discovered in Dover.

Globalisation is not a new phenomenon. In the mid-nineteenth century telegraph wires were laid across the Atlantic Ocean and steam ships greatly increased the speed with which people and goods transited the global empires of Britain and America, France, the Netherlands, Spain and Belgium. But at that time, while vast quantities of money and goods moved around freely, there were no passports and so people also moved with much greater ease between territories than they do or can today. If you had the money for the passage you could come to Britain if a colonial farmer had put you off your lands in Southern Africa. But today while we expect goods and money to travel freely, people must remain in their country of origin unless they are extremely rich, in which case they will be welcomed with open arms. And yet there are more refugees, more stateless people than there have ever been, more people scattered to the winds.

I was asked last weekend whether it would matter if the Anglican Communion broke into pieces, whether the unity of

Christians in the North with Christians in the South matters enough in the large scheme of things for a bishop to be prevented from taking his appointed see. I refer to the recent events concerning the see of Reading, and the echo of earlier events in the consecration of a bishop in the diocese of New Hampshire. In the context of a global empire which excludes more people from the Commonwealth of prosperity and the good life than it includes, the communion of Christians between North and South is no small thing. It is certainly not something to be given up lightly, for the symbolic assertion, through the consecration of a bishop, of Western freedoms and liberalities with regard to long-established ecclesial norms. Through our radical embrace of the Gospel of freedom we in the North are in the process of throwing off such norms. But the predominantly agrarian communities of developing nations still retain them. And for some Anglican churches, in places such as Nigeria, it would be a matter even of life and death were they to espouse the kind of liberal freedoms which we in the West increasingly espouse.

For Christians, our citizenship is not finally of one country, or even of one superstate – it is of heaven and not of earth. Our belonging to the kingdom of God as citizens is not analogous to our nationality as citizens. There are no border guards or immigration controls in the kingdom fashioned and brought near by our Risen and Ascended Lord. Global communion between Christians – full recognition of ministry and Eucharist, conferences between bishops and exchanges between congregations and dioceses – these are not incidentals to our being Church. They are a central feature of our belief that we are not finally defined by our status as citizens of particular countries, that our membership of the communion of saints is of more significance, a truer source of dignity, fellowship and freedom than our membership of territorial states defined by borders and fences and passport controls. To work as I have done for Anglican churches on the other side of the world, to have Anglican Christians as lifelong friends – who are from other cultures and live in other climate zones and nation states – is a tremendous gift. And it is a gift which we in this local church also enjoy by the membership and visitation of our church of families and individuals from so many places around the world – Uganda, South Africa, Australia, the United States, Canada, Malaysia, Kenya, and so on.

Christian communion across national borders transcends cultural and national identities – it represents the most powerful challenge that we could mount to the division of the world between rich and poor, between those whose animals enjoy shelter, clean water and fulsome protein and those whose children die for want of these things. Economic globalisation is a cruel perversion of the international communion of the kind which the Christian Church, including the Anglican Church, has sought to sustain in the post-colonial era.

The idea of global citizenship is a chimera – we are in truth being drawn into a global economy founded upon radical injustice, the threat and often the reality of war, and relations of increasing economic compulsion between rich and poor. Global Christian communion, however, is already a reality. It is no small thing. It deserves that we be prepared to make sacrifices to maintain it, even sacrifices of our freedom. St Paul frequently reminds the Corinthian Christians, who were the most free sexually and in other ways of any of the early Christians, that they should not use their freedom in such a way as to offend their brothers and sisters in Christ, and that charity comes before the assertion of the right of freedom.

Christ has indeed abolished the law but in its place he puts something far more demanding and more precious – he makes peace, peace to those who are far off and peace to those who are near for through the Spirit we all have access to the Father: 'So then you are no longer strangers and aliens but you are citizens with the saints and members of the household of God, built upon the foundation of the apostles and prophets with Christ Jesus as the cornerstone' (Ephesians 2:20).

Only through the communion of saints can the false humanistic vision of freedom – as freedom to colonise, control and consume the labour, lands and species of other parts of the world – be critiqued and resisted. Our citizenship, our fellowship and our security rest not upon credit cards, logos and patents, or passport controls, guns and threats of war. Christian communion is a precious thing, 'as precious as the oil of blessing dripping down on the beard of Aaron' (Ps. 133:2), as the Psalmist puts it. We should not easily cast aside this communion, either locally or globally. It will stand when the current global economic empire has bitten the dust.

27. Health, Safety and Salvation

October 2007

Honour your father and your mother that your days may be long in the land the Lord your God is giving you.

Exodus 20:12

The hubris of the modern legislator is astonishing. In this year's Queen's Speech the government announced dozens of new laws on everything from wayward youths to climate change but this same government has passed hundreds of new laws in the last ten years. Do we see a nation that is more just or more law abiding as a result? Far from it. Included in the Queen's Speech were a number of new laws on law and order, and terrorism, about which John Reid announced that the intent was that security would reach from government and the courts to people's living rooms. But this frightening vision of an invasive state rampant in its powers to scrutinise our lives does nothing to conform our hearts and minds to the prior claim that our neighbours have on our lives, or to create real peace in British communities. For Christians the claims of justice do not begin from the threat of punishment – divine or human, judicial or military – nor even from the all-seeing eye of God or the CCTV camera.

The problem is in our larger vision of what it is to be British, and to be human. The government constantly legislates to prevent harms but rarely seems able to promote a vision of the good life or positive justice, either at home or in its foreign policy. One of the worst examples of this understanding of politics as the prevention of harms was in a story I read this week about the Health and Safety Executive taking the National Trust to court because one of the trees in the ancient oak forest of Dunham Massey in Cheshire fell on a child in high winds three years ago in a freak accident. The Trust care for literally millions of trees but if the HSE gets its way none of us will be able to walk under them anymore if there's even a hint of wind. And yet we go to the wild, to the forest, to places of beauty and the sublime because they are not tamed, and in their wondrous natural power we enjoy them because we do not control them. Instead they give us a sense of the awe and majesty of creation and of the Creator who in wisdom has set the earth on its foundations and whose divine nature is manifest in the intricate order of every community of species, whether an oak forest or a salmon river.

The first point about the Ten Commandments, too, is that we do not make them. Think for a moment about how they are received. Moses is not sitting with a quill pen in an Egyptian city; he is not even in a tent encamped among the Israelites. No; he has climbed the great Mount Sinai in the desert – he is in the wilderness without a mobile phone or GPS or even a compass and OS map. And after days on the mountain he comes back down with a divine map, God's plan for human life, in the form of two tablets of stone.

What do these commands represent? The distillation of the wisdom of an ancient nomadic tribe? The law code of one of the first civilisations to actually write anything down? No; they are God's laws, and they affirm that there is no true life, no good life which is not directed to the love and worship of God. And the commandment we have before us today affirms that there is no life which is not received as a gift, from parents, and from God. And so: 'Honour your father and your mother that your days may be long in the land the Lord your God is giving you' (Exod. 20:12).

This commandment is pivotal since it comes between the commands concerned with human duties towards God and human duties towards life which is not divine. And its message is that those who do not honour their father and mother shall not live long in the land. To put this another way, those who fail to honour their roots are unlikely to be well rooted in the land or to enjoy its fruits for long. Edmund Burke, in reflecting on the

French Revolution, expressed the same thought this way: 'people will not look towards posterity when they fail to reflect on past generations.'[28]

We live in a culture which takes little or no thought for the morrow. Burke's suggestion is that this failure to care for the future welfare of people and planet is a consequence of our failure to reflect on the past, to know whence we have come. The reason why we think like this is because we are trained by our culture to imagine that society, and even we ourselves, are human creations and that through our choices – of friends, partners, homes, clothes, cars, holidays – we make ourselves. And not only do we make ourselves but we decide, we legislate for, we *make* what is right and wrong. In our culture right and wrong depend on our choices and relationships. Coldplay put this rather well in a song from a recent album:

> What if there was no lie
> Nothing wrong, nothing right
> What if there was no time
> And no reason, or rhyme
> What if you should decide
> That you don't want me there by your side.

If right and wrong are just sentiments, passing emotions, feelings we can't explain, choices we can't justify, and if identity is something we make up from our dreams, the idea that someone else created us is deeply problematic. As Philip Larkin famously put it,

> They fuck you up, your mum and dad.
> They may not mean to, but they do.
> They fill you with the faults they had
> And add some extra, just for you.

The implication is that if we controlled our own destiny – if we somehow made ourselves – we would not be in such a mess. And the further implication is that the only relationships that truly affirm our identity are relationships we freely choose.

---

28   Edmund Burke, *Reflections on the Revolution in France* (London: James Dodsley, 1790), 164.

Parents give us birth. And their presence in our lives is a constant reminder that we receive life not as a possession but as a gift. We did not intend ourselves into being. Analogously we don't obey the commands because we wrote them, or we judge them to be wise, nor even that we fear some horrendous punishment if we don't do them. We believe that they point us to the good life – the life God intended us to live – because they come to us from the God who made us.

And here the order of the commandments is significant – we do not make gods because we receive life from God as a gift. We don't abuse the name of God because even to name God is to overstate things – we receive God's life but we do not control the God who made us. We do not control time, time is ordered to God and to the worship of God. And then the fourth command-ment – we do not make ourselves. We receive life as a gift from our parents, just as we receive time as a gift, and the name of God as a gift, and are commanded to worship truly in recognition of this gift.

And the placing of this command also suggests that all our other relationships will be built on how we negotiate our parental relationships – if we can love God then we can love our parents, and if God forgives us then we can forgive our parents for messing us up, and if we can do that then how much more will we be able to forgive our neighbours also. And if we can forgive our neighbours we are less likely to want to kill them, steal from them, be unfaithful to them, or covet their belongings.

Some suggest that these five 'human' laws are the really significant heritage of the commandments and the religious laws are of less significance for society – that human law is written on these laws and that it is the solid foundation which gives the law power over our lives. But nothing could be further from the truth. Law alone does not save – as St Paul says the law is at best a tutor, which can teach us that we stand in need of grace but which cannot ultimately redeem.

Jeremiah was surely right when he suggested that in the days of the messiah God would write God's laws on human hearts or, in another form of the metaphor, replace a heart of stone with a heart of flesh – the laws were the heart of Israel. But the law that God makes new and fulfils in Christ is a law written on the heart not on tablets of stone. And this recognition also changes how we think about these laws. The laws before us are actually pretty vague – they do not give us cases, they invite interpretation and argument and reflection.

Thus the law about respecting parents is not an absolute law – it does not mean never disobey, never go your own way. But it means for the adult children to whom it is addressed – never forget that you are creatures, that you first received life so that you might in turn give it. It means in our own time that family is more central to life than the market or the state. Our society is currently obsessed with 'out of control' children and no doubt many of the laws announced this week will be designed to restrain them – but no one asks 'why?' What has destroyed stable communities and stable families if not the idol of the market, and the idea that for something to be worthwhile it must have a money price? Time for parenting is unpaid – it is not valued by the market, and yet it is priceless.

The story of the Ten Commandments is the foundational story of Jewish and Christian culture. We forget its meaning at our peril. And yet this fourth and pivotal commandment ends not with a threat of punishment but of blessing – do this, live like this, and your days will be long in the land the Lord gives. To put this another way, our actions do have consequences. How we live does make a difference. True worship, responsible, restrained work, respect for the past and our elders, peaceableness, fidelity, thankfulness for what we have rather than covetousness for what we do not – societies ordered around these things will not breed growing numbers of violent criminals and fraudsters. Societies that uphold and train their citizens in these positive goods will not need to legislate to prevent their citizens from harming one another. Following these laws does bring a blessing and however much we may lament when bad things happen to good people we should also remember, and give thanks, how more often it is that good things happen to good people.

Thanksgiving – for the gift of life – counting our blessings – these are not the habits of a commodity-obsessed culture but they are the practices that the law requires and that the Spirit of Christ would write on our hearts.

28. Inequality and the Good Society

He hath showed you, O people, what is good; and what doth the LORD require of you, but to do justly, and to love mercy, and to walk humbly with your God?

Micah 6:8

Faith without works is dead.

James 2:20

Last Thursday I went to see my GP. I had a small skin rash which had troubled me for some time and all my traditional remedies had failed. I cycled to the surgery on a warm sunny day, sat outside while I waited looking at the trees in the garden of a large house in Trinity across the road from the surgery and thought what a good thing the Victorians had done in laying out this particular Edinburgh suburb. The doctor was someone I had not met before and he told me he only worked there one morning a week. The rest of the time he worked in Oxgangs and I said to him 'so you come here for some light relief', and he said 'yes, the diseases of the affluent are generally easier to fix.' And he was right. He prescribed a tub of cream which seems to be working rather better than the olive oil I had been experimenting with before.

The visit and the conversation brought home to me, in a powerful way, the truth just below the surface in every one of Ian Rankin's Rebus novels: I and he live in a city, Edinburgh, which is scandalously unequal in income and which is tragically divided by health, educational and criminological outcomes. My wife Jill met Ian Rankin at the Edinburgh Book Festival earlier this month. I have never met Richard Wilkinson but he is an author I would really like to shake warmly by the hand. He has not written any crime novels but he is responsible for an impressive stream of academic papers and a couple of books on the subject of health inequality. He is Professor of Social Epidemiology at the University of Nottingham and he has made it his life's work to expose with hard empirical data the links between ill health, crime and income inequality. The first part of the story he tells draws on data that show that, in all OECD countries including Britain, there is a very weak statistical correlation indeed between average rises in income and better health outcomes. We are so accustomed to the mantra that economic growth is good for all, rich and poor, or that a rising tide lifts all boats, that this is surprising. But his data are unbeatably convincing.

The next part of the picture Wilkinson paints is that there is a very strong relationship between mortality rates and income inequality within postcodes or zip codes across the US, the UK and Europe. The data reveal consistently and unequivocally that the more unequal a society in income, the lower the average death rate. To put this another way, what Wilkinson shows is that even the rich in unequal countries do not live as long as the rich in more equal countries. His data also reveal something which is perhaps less surprising, which is that the difference between life expectancy of the richest and the poorest in unequal societies such as Britain can be up to 20 years.

Wilkinson's findings are not limited to health. He has done similar studies of the relationship between inequality, crime and violence and found again direct and incontestably similar connections. Those cities and societies which are marked by deep relative income inequality – Chicago or Johannesburg or, closer to home, Glasgow or London – have higher murder rates and higher rates of violent crime while societies and cities where inequality is relatively low – Oslo or Singapore – have correlatively low rates of violent crime and murder.

Wilkinson is the kind of scholar I admire. He even makes me think I might have chosen the right career in academia because he puts his scholarly knowledge and skill to work in forensically precise and yet passionate writing in which he tells a powerful moral story which challenges received wisdom. As he puts it in his recent book *The Spirit Level*,

> The relation between violence and inequality appears to be part of a more general tendency for the quality of social relationships to be less good in more unequal societies. As well as experiencing higher rates of violence, people in more unequal societies tend to trust each other less and are less likely to be involved in community life. There are lower levels of social capital; hostility levels seem to be higher and there is almost certainly more discrimination against minorities and against women.[29]

The epistle of James is one of the more challenging and controversial epistles in the New Testament. Its inclusion in the canon was even questioned by Luther who disliked the extent to which it seemed to require that works must accompany faith. I am glad no one listened to him since when we read this passage in the context of what I have just been saying we come to see straight away what James means when he says faith without works is dead. The passage is full of wisdom – discrimination between rich and poor is a sign of an evil mind, it produces evil thoughts. This is strong language indeed. But there is truth here, deep truth and we hear echoes in Wilkinson – unequal societies are those where rich judge the poor and the poor dislike and distrust the rich – inequality produces wicked thoughts and wicked thoughts produce disease and violence.

And then we read that most Christians in the churches to whom James writes are poor and not rich, and that they are being persecuted by the rich who drag them into the law courts. James reminds them that whether poor or rich they are under one and the same command of love; to love one's neighbour as oneself means that no partiality can be shown. And James reminds them that all the moral law is interconnected – it is no good being sexually righteous while thinking evil thoughts about the poor and honouring only the rich. There is a holism here which again Wilkinson would recognise.

---

29 Richard Wilson and Kate Pickett, *The Spirit Level: Why More Equal Societies Almost Always Do Better* (London: Penguin, 2009), 32.

And so we come to the conclusion Luther hated: *faith without works is dead.*

One of the strongest articles of faith in British politics these last thirty years is that rising affluence, greater rewards for the successful, and reduced efforts to redistribute wealth, make for a better and a healthier society. But the reality is otherwise. Without works of love and charity, without myriad shared projects in which communities and individuals work towards what faith only believes, our society is set on a sorry, even a wicked road.

Palestine in the time of Jesus was a society that was even further than ours down the road of inequality, ill health and violence – indeed Palestine then was not so different in terms of prejudice, disease and violence from Palestine today. It had been ruled by the Romans for decades and the regions of Tyre and Sidon, and the Decapolis, had suffered particularly cruelly at the hands of garrisons of Roman legionnaires who had slaughtered thousands of the local inhabitants in the decade preceding Christ's journeys there.

In the Gospel before us today we have this memorable story of the Gentile Syrophoenecian woman who seeks Christ's aid in delivering her daughter from a demon (Mark 7:25–30). Christ as a Jew was not expected by his Jewish disciples to have anything to do with Gentiles, and yet on a number of occasions he deals with Gentiles and even declares on a couple of occasions that they had more faith than his own people.

In this story too we find a Gentile woman who is courageous and won't take no for an answer. Jesus uses what is for us a scandalous analogy – comparing her request for help from a Jewish rabbi to that of a dog taking food from a child's plate – and like Jesus on many other occasions she parries the challenge back with wit and grace and so provokes Christ to deliver her child from the demon. As Dominic Crossan has pointed out most of those who suffered from these kinds of conditions, and from ill health, in Palestine at the time of Christ were people who had become poor and often landless because of the oppressive imperial economy of Rome. In healing disease and delivering the demon oppressed, Christ was not only challenging physical illness – he was addressing the physical and psychological symptoms of the deep violence and pathology of a group of people who had become subject to the capricious and violent rule of imperial Rome.

It is often said that Christ preached and practised the kingdom and Paul and Peter invented the Church but this in my view is a cheap shot. The early Church was indeed a place where Jew and Gentile both worshipped God despite their deep historic divisions of creed and race. And it was a place where rich and poor worshipped side by side. Now we know from the New Testament itself that these divisions still persisted inside the Church but we also know that the apostles' teaching was that these divisions were not to characterise the people of God. And we know furthermore that in this witness the Christians were on the whole successful – it was precisely because they established egalitarian communities in which the poor were well treated and the rich were not accorded greater respect, and because they refused to worship the gods who sustained the inequality and violence of empire, that they were persecuted, rich and poor alike, by Rome.

Faith in the market, faith in riches, faith in extreme wealth are forms of idolatry that are displacing collective solidarity in works of love and mercy in our society today. And the collective service of these idols is as surely leading to the civilisational decline and moral corruption of our society as the obsessive pursuit of luxury, pornography and violence accompanied Rome's decline and fall. Like the early Christians, we find ourselves in the midst of a society increasingly at odds with the divinity of justice and the pursuit of equity. In this situation we are called more than ever to seek in our own lives, in the workplace, and in our shared service in the Church 'to do justly, to love mercy and to walk humbly with our God' (Micah 6: 8).

29. Arms and Ploughshares

October 2002

Render unto Caesar the things that are Caesars, and unto God the things which are God's.

Matthew 22:21

Today in Washington, DC, two kinds of fear haunt the land. First there is the fear of international terrorists which is driving the war on terror, and the plan to invade and subdue Iraq and install a military-style American-led government after the model of the McArthur administration of Japan at the end of the Second World War. Second there is the fear of a lone gunman – possibly working with an accomplice driver – who has been picking off individual suburban residents at random for three weeks now at gas stations, malls and other locations. So far ten people have died. Spy planes sweep the skies above Washington, DC, Maryland and Virginia looking for a needle in a haystack – a driver of a white van who occasionally stops, opens the window of his van and shoots a victim with a single bullet from his hunter's rifle. Meanwhile the more than four million residents of the region drive their children to school, cower behind their cars when filling them at gas stations, and confine themselves and their children as much as possible to staying indoors.

At first sight these events are not evidently connected, the one concerning militant opponents of the United States emanating from or located in the Middle East and the other a domestic criminal of a chillingly wicked profile. But think again. Both threats are connected to the deadly trade in weapons which drives forward such a large part of the American economy, and of other arms-exporting countries, including Britain, Belgium, South Africa, and Israel. Saddam Hussein was a principal beneficiary of this trade in the 1970s and 1980s. Britain and America, anxious to back this oil-rich and secular Gulf state, sold billions of dollars of weapons to Saddam Hussein, and the volume greatly increased once he took on the new Islamic and anti-Western government of Iran in the Iran–Iraq war. Al Qaeda also received American assistance in acquiring an extensive range of weaponry as it was a principal opponent of the Russian occupation of Afghanistan, which the US in the 1980s sought any means to undermine. And what about that Washington sniper? America not only liberally trades its arms with dictators and terrorists in every part of the globe; it also has a vast and notoriously lax internal trade in arms, sustained by the fiction that the American Constitution supports the right of every individual citizen to bear arms. In fact the constitution only supported this right for citizens who were also members of recognised local militias but this reading is disputed by the gun-slinging advocates who speak for the powerful gun lobby, the National Rifle Association. Speaking on Radio 4 on Thursday one of their spokespersons defended the freedom of Americans to carry guns by arguing that it helped to keep burglaries down, and by pointing out that only one per cent of the guns currently in circulation in the United States had been used in crimes. When James Naughtie, in an interview on the *Today* programme, asked how much this one per cent amounted to he received an astonishing reply: two million.

Ever since the end of the Second World War the churches in America and Europe have regularly chastised governments and arms manufacturers for the proliferating global arms trade, and the tide of human suffering that this trade in weapons of death brings in its wake. A 2001 report to the General Assembly of the Church of Scotland points out that 23 million deaths have occurred in wars since 1945, most of these in countries in the 'impoverished South', and most of the deaths being of civilians rather than military personnel. They cite a UN Report which estimates that for every 200 million pounds spent by a developing country on arms, infant mortality increases by 20 deaths in 1,000 births, 14 fewer adults out of a hundred attain literacy and life expectancy reduces by three to four years. The report goes on to criticise the UK government not only for its failure to end the sale of so many deadly weapons to countries in the South – whose citizens have much more urgent need of clean water, drains and teachers – but also for the continuing government support for the arms trade. The level and quality of this support has actually grown in the last five years to the point that salespersons from some of Britain's largest arms exporters are now to be found seconded to the staff of embassies and high commissions in countries where it is thought their presence may enhance Britain's business opportunities. This even exceeds the kind of thing which went on under the Thatcher government in the 1980s which was highlighted by the discovery that the British High Commissioner to Malaysia, (Sir) Charles Spreckley, had orchestrated a deal whereby arms were given to Malaysia as part of a development aid package in exchange for lucrative contracts for British engineering companies to build the Pergau Dam.

But the Pergau Dam affair – which took place when I lived in Malaysia – was only the tip of a very large iceberg. According to Samuel Brittan in a Royal Society of Arts lecture on 'The Ethics and Economics of the Arms Trade', more than 350 million pounds of taxpayers' money is devoted to direct subsidies to the arms export industry. And other kinds of subsidy include the vast budget of the Ministry of Defence every year for military supplies of all kinds, and direct subsidies to arms production deals such as the Eurofighter project and Challenger II tank, none of which would have gone ahead without direct government investment. Brittan also records another and murkier form of subsidy in the form of the Al Yammamah arms for oil deal with one of the most repressive governments in the world, the fiefdom of Saudi Arabia. Under this deal Britain was able to create a market for the Tornado Aircraft which is said to have shored up 19,000 jobs in the early 1990s.

It is the claim that the arms trade also provides jobs which allows Members of Parliament as well as government ministers to defend this diversion of taxpayers' money into the production of weapons of death and destruction. Brittan quotes the estimated number of workers in the weapons-production industries as 90,000, which is around one-third of one per cent of UK employees; the Ministry of Defence claims up to 400,000 are involved directly and indirectly in the arms industry. If Brittan is right it is hard to see how such a tiny proportion of jobs can be used to justify the large government subsidies to the weapons industries. Nor can it explain why government officials and military representatives, at public expense, attend so many trade fairs to promote the sale of arms, such as the trade fair in South Africa this weekend which will have among its customers members of the government of Saddam Hussein. The double standards in the context of the present government's declared commitment to eradicating poverty in the South and to backing the 'war on terror' are breathtaking, leaving aside its now rather tattered claims to an ethical foreign policy. Ever since the government agreed to the sale of planes and Land Rovers used in the repression – and recently the horrific and mindless destruction – of parts of the island of East Timor by the occupying Indonesian army, the claims made in the 1997 Labour Party Manifesto that it would not sell arms which were likely to be used in the repression of civilians have looked distinctly implausible. Samuel Brittan does, however, record some progress in government efforts to make the whole business more transparent. The Blair administration has initiated annual reports in which all licences for arms exports are recorded and has pressed for similar levels of transparency across the European Union.

One of the most pernicious aspects of the arms trade is the extent to which the government, through the Export Credit Guarantee Department, actually takes on the risk of selling many of these arms in the first place. The ECGD in effect bankrolls a good many arms contracts between impoverished governments in the South and UK arms manufacturers and dealers. The ECGD pays the firms for the arms exports, and then the countries concerned must pay back the UK government. As a consequence hundreds of millions of pounds of debt has accumulated between the UK government and governments in the

South directly relating to arms sales. Much of it is never likely to be paid back, but in the meantime the citizens of many of these countries suffer cutbacks in essential social programmes to pay interest on these dubious loans.

Brittan proposed a number of things which would make a big difference to the UK involvement in the arms trade. The single most effective change would be to end the extraordinary practice of using taxpayers' money to bankroll and subsidise arms exports. Another would be to allow the Department for International Development (DFID) to scrutinise, and where necessary veto, arms export licences to impoverished nations in the South. A further step would be to increase the transparency of the reports on arms exports so that in every case they indicate the end user of weapons' exports so that, for example, there will be no repeat of the sale of arms to the repressive regime of Robert Mugabe in Zimbabwe in 1998 and 1999. Brittan finally suggests that the National Audit Office should be invited to provide a complete and impartial audit of all UK arms sales and their costs to the taxpayer.

None of these measures, however, are advanced in the government's long-awaited bill called the Arms Export Control and Non-Proliferation Bill. The bill as published does offer more legal controls which will hopefully enable the government to ensure that arms end up with the users to whom they are officially sold. But it does nothing to reform, let alone abolish, the morally hazardous ECGD subsidies. It allows no parliamentary scrutiny of arms export licences. And it does nothing to strengthen the monitoring of the use of arms beyond the point of sale. Furthermore it still does not prevent UK arms dealers dealing in arms from other countries without recourse to official licensing procedures, including even other countries in the European Union.

The most fundamental point in all this is really the diversion of taxes paid by voters for the subsidy of a trade which has such vicious and inhuman outcomes as the arms trade. The funding of the military by taxation has a very long history, but so too does Christian resistance to it. Jesus was one day arraigned by an unusual alliance of pro-Roman Herodians and anti-Roman Pharisees and asked what he thought about paying taxes to the emperor. The poll tax – as it was known – was levied on everyone living in the empire and the first claim upon the empire's budget was the maintenance of its vast armies of legionnaires who kept the empire subdued under the harsh rule of Rome and shored up its borders. Jesus saw the question coming and characteristically turned it around. First he asked them to show him the coin – the denarius– which was used to pay the tax. This was a nice piece of irony in itself for the implication is that Jesus himself did not carry such coins. When his religious disputants produced the coin he asked whose head was upon it, and it was as they declared, the head of Caesar. And so the occasion for his brilliant reply to their question: 'render unto Caesar the things that are Caesar's, and unto God the things which are God's' (Mark 12:17), against which his opponents could find no effective reply.

The answer has been as hotly debated since the original debating contest in which it was first given. Does Jesus mean to support the empire by suggesting the poll tax should be paid? Or did Jesus on the contrary hold the empire in such contempt that he would not even carry its coinage, let alone pay it to the empire in taxes? Given his death at the hands of the representative of the emperor for sedition, the latter position seems more plausible than the former. Radical Christians both in the early Church and in more recent times have therefore not only consistently refused military service of any kind, but have opposed use of any monies they give to the state for purposes of warfare.

However the most radical witness against the weapons industry has come from those brave women in the Ploughshares movement who have damaged fighter jets and ventured into nuclear submarine bases at considerable personal cost and often with the consequence of many weeks or even months in prison.

And there is no doubt that this kind of direct action is highly effective at exposing the lie that the possession of weapons, let alone their sale to other states who may one day be our enemy, is a source of human security. Equally effective though is the Christian witness to practices of peacemaking and non-violent conflict resolution.

One of the most wonderful things to have come out of the ending of apartheid in South Africa has been the bringing to justice – through the Truth and Reconciliation Process – of hundreds of people in the apartheid regimes' police and armed forces who killed and maimed and terrorised the black population on its behalf. These individuals have had to face their victims – often disabled if still living – and more often the families of those they have killed, and confess the true horror and extent of their crimes. They have done this in the knowledge that public confession and contrition will mean a state pardon. And some families of victims have been unable to forgive them. But many have, and the process itself has done a great deal to restore a sense of justice to broken and persecuted communities without the use of coercive violence.

Restorative justice does work and is proven to do so because it involves the traditional Christian practices of confession of sin between oppressor or criminal and victim. This process of confession is often more of a punishment – and more reforming of character and behaviour – than anonymous time done inside.

Yes, Christians can and must openly and loudly condemn the arms trade. But equally they must show in their own lives that they are peacemakers, that they embrace the practices of non-violence, and of non-violent conflict resolution. Security does not come from the bomb, let alone from a hand gun, despite what the NRA tells the people of America. America locks up more people in its jails than any other nation on the planet as a proportion of its population. Only Stalin's Gulag and Hitler's concentration camps exceeded the proportion – nearly one per cent – of the population which America bangs up in its violent and drug-ridden penitentiaries. This is a country which has allowed the gun to reduce many of its own cities to a state of armed terror while its President continues to proclaim that it is a 'freedom-loving' nation. It is hardly surprising that this same country sponsors the proliferation of small arms and weapons of mass destruction all over the globe.

In the end the only real security is to be found when neighbour does not fear neighbour, when not only the technologies of surveillance and war are banished from our streets and from government accounting sheets, but when we remove the fear of the one who is different from us from our own hearts. Christians invoke the divine Spirit as the one who can replace a spirit of fear with a spirit of love. There are those who will say it is utopian to expect that such a spirit can ever be manifest in society at large. But Christians are also called to live in hope, hope that the promised reign of peace will come on earth, when the lion will lie down with the lamb and nation will no longer take up sword against nation, and instead beat their spears into pruning forks and their shields into ploughshares.

30. The Divine Bias toward Children

June 2007

And Abraham stretched forth his hand, and took the knife to slay his son. And the angel of the LORD called unto him out of heaven, and said, Abraham, Abraham: and he said, Here am I. And he said, Lay not thine hand upon the lad, neither do thou any thing unto him: for now I know that thou fearest God, seeing thou hast not withheld thy son, thine only son from me.

Genesis 22:11–12

The story of the intended sacrifice of Isaac by Abraham (Genesis 22) is what feminist scholar Phyllis Trible calls a 'text of terror'. It is, on one reading, a story which tells of a man who is so obsessed by his religious beliefs that he is prepared to kill his only son in sacrifice according to what he believes to be the command of his God. On this reading Abraham is worse than a suicide bomber. He is not prepared to sacrifice his own life to his terrible faith; instead he believes God requires that he kill the son for whom he and Sarah had waited so long and whom they treasured above all things.

It is hard to imagine the terror, to say nothing of the incomprehension, that Isaac must have felt when his father tied him on the altar and raised a knife to kill him. It is even harder to imagine what he told his wife Sarah about the incident when he eventually returned home with Isaac physically but surely not mentally unscarred. And yet this story is one of the foundational stories in the history of the Abrahamic faiths, embraced for its religious power by Jews and Muslims as well as Christians.

Richard Holloway, who in his darker moments tends to believe that religion is a force for ill rather than good in the world, finds in this text a powerful exemplar of his suspicion that religion makes us bad. For Holloway Abraham is a crazed child-killer who is little better than the monster portrayed by Anthony Hopkins in *The Silence of the Lambs*.

The Danish philosopher Søren Kierkegaard had a different reading of it.[30] For the great Dane the passage poses the central conundrum in human life: is an action or a practice good because God makes it so or do we only know about goodness from judging the consequences of our actions? For Kierkegaard, if the latter is true then we have no need of God, since we can know and pursue the good without God.

For Kierkegaard the story indicates that the good is not obvious or self-evident. Only those who take a leap of faith are able, like Abraham, to pursue the command of God where it leads. And only the faithful will understand that their attempts to pursue the good need guidance and undergirding by the mysterious power and providence of God.

There is another crucial insight in what Kierkegaard tells us about this story. We are encouraged by our technological civilisation to imagine that when we are in control of our lives, and base our actions and choices on our careful estimates of their consequences, then we are pursuing the good as God intends. We live in a culture which is so devoted to the statistical estimation of consequences that there is no good which may not be sacrificed on the altar of cost benefit calculations.

A good example of the effects of these sums was raised by Archbishop Rowan Williams in a lecture in 2005 on the formation of children in which he called for the banning of advertisements aimed at under-12s on TV and elsewhere. The government of Sweden has already done this and it has been welcomed by parents. However in the UK the response of business corporations is the predictable one that it is an unjustifiable infringement on their freedom to market and sell their products. The difficulty with this argument is that this freedom comes at the price of the loss of freedom of those whose desires

---

30 Søren Kierkegaard, *Fear and Trembling*, trans. Alastair Hannay (London: Penguin, 1985).

are misshapen by the incredibly powerful medium of modern advertising, a medium which young children especially just do not have the rational faculties to resist easily.

Recently UNICEF published a report on the state of children in developed societies. Its authors found troubling evidence that the welfare of children is declining in the two countries, Britain and the United States, which are most prone to put the interests of their corporations ahead of children and parents.[31]

But it is not only government and business corporations which are at fault. Parents in wealth- and work-obsessed Britain and America are also colluding with the displacement of the traditional pleasures of childhood – family meals, walks in the park and the countryside, games of tag, fairy stories, sports, music making – with electronic entertainment and other kinds of commercialised activities. There is less space in a commercialised society for children to be children and so to be formed in the kinds of desires and practices which will enable them to live responsible and ultimately holy lives as adults.

And there are other losses of freedom for children in contemporary culture. The constant media attention to paedophiles creates fear in many parents who will not let their children go out on their own. Equally, under-supervised children in some parts of our cities roam the streets and get into trouble – like the children who I am told were responsible for stealing three bicycle wheels and other parts off my family's bikes a few months ago. Cars are also a cause of a loss of freedom. I can remember going off cycling on my own from metroland into the North Downs in Kent in my early teens; it was possible to cycle for miles on roads in those days without feeling threatened by speeding cars. Nowadays it is rare to go on a bike journey on road where speeding cars or trucks do not come too close, or a frustrated driver in a traffic jam does not hurl abuse.

As a culture we are increasingly sacrificing social peace and the flourishing of future generations on the altar of the market and consumerism. The Moloch of our day – what Gerard Manley

---

31 *Child Poverty in Perspective: An Overview of Child Well-being in Rich Countries* (Florence: Innocenti Research Centre and UNICEF, 2007).

Hopkins called the infection of trade – is no less an idol than the Moloch of Abraham's time. Its demands are just as insidious, though its sacrifices less evidently bloody, although 3,500 deaths and tens of thousands of serious injuries every year – and the fear of crossing or even playing on the streets suffered by our children – is a bloody testimony to the idolatry of the car in Britain.

The terrifying story of Abraham and Isaac is ultimately a story about the contest between the God of Israel and the idols of other cultures in the ancient Near East where child sacrifices were not uncommon. Abraham is represented in comparison to these other religious peoples as just as devoted as they to his God for he is prepared to follow the command of God wherever it takes him. But when the occasion approaches God provides an alternative sacrifice and saves the child.

The great story of Abraham and Isaac is a bit like a fairy tale. Tales of abusive adults, dark desires, evil deeds, horrendous monsters, and of the courage and persistence in goodness which are required to resist them have an enduring effect in the formation of children, as Bruno Bettelheim argues in *The Uses of Enchantment*.[32] The world of the fairy tale is one in which conventional values and virtues are constantly held up to challenge and scrutiny and where heroic deeds in the face of terror are performed by the most unlikely kinds of heroes.

Abraham too is an unlikely hero, and in this story he at first looks more like a monster. But the story becomes a tale of providence overcoming wickedness, of harmful desire being reordered by divine compassion, and of the love of a father for his child being ultimately vindicated as divinely blessed.

Christ also sets children, and a concern for children, at the heart of the Gospel, suggesting that childlike trust is a better exemplar of faith in the kingdom than adult suspicion. And on a famous occasion when the disciples tried to prevent people bringing children to him for blessing he suggests that they, and not the disciples, are true exemplars of the kingdom because of their child-like faith (Luke 18:16–17).

---

32 Bruno Bettelheim, *The Uses of Enchantment: The Meaning and Importance of Fairy Tales* (London: Penguin, 1976).

When we first came to live in Edinburgh after a sojourn of five years in Malaysia in 1989 we found it to be a particularly unwelcoming place for children. I well remember one of our children saying to us – 'why is it that adults only talk to children here when they want to tell them off?' This was a highly observant comment from someone who had spent much of her childhood in a culture where children were constantly welcomed into adult society – in conversation, at evenings out, and in restaurants. Things have improved somewhat since then but there can be no question that the threats to childhood in our culture are still very real and that they are the reverse side of Christ's saying. Just as those who welcome children welcome God into their lives, so those who sacrifice the welfare of children to commercial profit and the desire for wealth are acting out a devotion to idols other than God.

If we in Britain were able to make the formation of children the central issue in our political deliberations our society would come closer to the kingdom of heaven than to Babylon, even though most of our fellow citizens no longer acknowledge Christ as Lord. Such a prioritisation would also commit us to a different vision of the future since it is children who will literally inherit the earth and who ought to be given the opportunity to live on a planet as rich in species and as stable in climate as that enjoyed by their parents.

I heard of a wonderful example of this kind of intergenerational responsibility at the AGM of Traidcraft in London last year. Paul Chandler, Traidcraft's Chief Executive, described how in a visit to a jute handicrafts project in Dakka, India, he asked the mostly women workers what difference thirty years of fair trading with Traidcraft had made to their lives. They were after all still living in very simple huts with few of the comforts and daily conveniences we enjoy in our homes. And they said to him that the difference regular payments for their handicrafts had made was that they had been able to afford school fees and because of that they had been able to give their children an education and so lift them out of poverty. And now their children had real jobs and were helping to support their parents. Traidcraft's new catalogue shows an expanding range of products – a lot of an average weekly shop can now be bought online from Traidcraft – and fair trade products are also now widely available from other companies. Traidcraft originated the model of fair trade in Britain as a Christian response to poverty, and its relationships with its producers are therefore long-term and sustainable. Long-term fair trade by Traidcraft is already having multigenerational effects on the children of fair trade producers.

The story of Abraham ultimately refused the child sacrifice practised by the old religions. And Christ – by upholding children as exemplars of the kingdom, and by going the way of the cross – resists the imperious sacrifices demanded from his people by the rulers of Galilee, Judea and Rome. Regulation and restriction of commercial advertising, and fair trade which resists poverty, are practices which enact the divine bias toward children that these biblical narratives reveal.

31. The Return of the Wolf

June 2007

I send you out as lambs among wolves.

Matthew 11:21–22

I was recently in Kuala Lumpur for the consecration of one of my former students as Bishop. The Cathedral of St Mary's, where I had served as a priest, had just been extended and a beautiful new second sanctuary added with a glass wall at the front looking out on a fountain with the city beyond. It all had a new coat of paint, new furniture in the Sunday school classes, new computers in the offices, and new cooker, fridge and work surfaces in the kitchen. And three weeks after the consecration, just as Dean Jason was leaving for a well-earned break in the UK, an exceptionally heavy rainstorm hit the city and its environs. The water that should have been trapped in the river catchment poured down off the hills, mostly denuded of trees. And the city's monsoon drains overflowed. The river runs close to the cathedral and it was for a couple of days under five feet of water, the worst flood since 1973. Large areas of Kuala Lumpur – which is set like Dunkeld at the meeting point of two rivers – were also flooded. But this was little consolation to the cathedral members who had worked hard to raise the money to extend and renew this historic building in the colonial heart of Kuala Lumpur. When the waters subsided there was a foot of foul mud in the church, much of it mixed with sewage, and as a result the newly painted walls are now sprouting moulds and fungus.

The residents of Hull, Sheffield and Doncaster were hit by similar sudden and devastating floods just a week after the flood in Kuala Lumpur. At the same time large parts of Australia, Africa, and the United States are experiencing exceptional droughts, high temperatures and forest fires. Hundreds of homes were burning in California back in April, an exceptionally early time for the seasonal forest fires to hit, and they spread over a much larger area than normal.

Last weekend two bishops of the Church of England suggested that the floods were the judgment of God on the hedonism of our culture. I think this is perhaps too literal a way of reading these events. But there is a sense in which – and perhaps this is what the bishops had in mind – the floods are a judgment on our civilisation as we consume more and more fossil fuels. Since 2000 our uses of them have gone up five per cent, year on year, despite the scientific warnings – and so the planet is literally heating up and extreme weather events become more common.

In our gospel this morning Jesus calls down a curse on three towns which had all witnessed to the many miracles of healing and deliverance that he performed in his ministry but whose people had mostly not received him as messiah. That Jesus should curse as well as bless is so shocking that the liberal compilers of our Revised Common Lectionary have actually tried to prevent us from reading the offending curses by keeping them out of the lectionary reading!

The attempt to manipulate the Scripture to fit our modern liberal sentiments is incredibly revealing for it shows that we as a civilisation no longer believe in something as old fashioned as judgment. But there are in fact two ways in which the disasters which have hit this small island in recent days are judgments.

First we are responsible as a country for a disproportionate amount of greenhouse gas emissions – our multinational corporations in their construction, drilling, mining, manufacturing and transportation activities around the world are responsible for roughly 10 per cent of global greenhouse gas emissions which is five times the greenhouse gases emitted by households and businesses within the UK itself. We have also, as a country, been in the greenhouse gas game longer than most – since 1750 we have emitted a larger quantity per head than any other country in the world.

James Lovelock calls global warming the revenge of Gaia. The Hebrew prophets read ecological calamity in an analogous way. The curse that polluted the lands of ancient Israel and led to the abandonment of towns like Jericho on the plains of ancient Israel was pollution from excessive irrigation which dragged the salts from under the soil and poisoned the land. Their laws warned them not to deep plough the fragile soils like the Egyptians, and not to enslave one another on large farms or in foreign wars, but their leaders neglected them and did all these things. And, the prophets say, the land itself rises up in protest. 'For they have sewn the wind and they shall reap the whirlwind' (Hos. 8:7).

And there is a second sense in which these events are a judgment. The main organiser of the medical students who perpetrated the terrorist attack on Glasgow airport last week is an Iraqi who was so angered by the wreckage left of the country where his parents still live that he decided to visit a judgment on the UK. Of course my intention is in no way to justify this terrible act of violence. But this act occurred in a terrible context. The results of a household survey conducted in Iraq last year were recently published in the medical journal *The Lancet* and it revealed that approximately one million Iraqis have met premature violent deaths since the start of the present Iraq War. One evil does not resolve another. But to claim – as the government have – that the war is about making Britain safe is mendacious to say the least in the light of the terror attacks on Britain whose stated motive – in the case of the London and Glasgow bombings – was said to be revenge for Britain's attack on Iraq. Once again the Bible, and more especially Jesus Christ, is prescient – 'he who lives by the sword dies by the sword' (Matt. 26:52).

There is nothing in the teachings of Jesus which could justify the decision of this country to go to war in Iraq, especially when we know that we went to war not to prevent war but for oil. If we did not already know this the Defence Minister of Australia actually came out with a statement last week in which he said that, yes, Australia was in Iraq because of oil and it would not be there if Iraq's principal export was sheep's wool.

Last week a British child, three years old, was kidnapped in Port Hartcourt. Port Hartcourt is an oil-exporting port in the heart of the Niger Delta. I have a Nigerian PhD student who is a Baptist pastor there and his congregation have been deeply affected by the violence of the region in the last ten years. That violence has been provoked by the oil industry which has ravaged the region with leaky pipes, constant gas flares which make it so hot people cannot sleep, lakes of crude oil bubbling out of the ground, and overland pipes rusting and leaking even as they pass through poor Ikbo villages. And the largest company behind this? Not a poor, ill-resourced African oil company but the Dutch and British imperial giant Shell Oil.[33]

My graduate student is exploring in his research how Nigerian Christians can witness peaceably in the middle of an ecological resource war and the strife it has provoked even among members of his own congregation.

Jesus commissioned his disciples with a word of warning: 'I send you out as lambs among wolves' (Luke 10:3). There is a proposal to bring wolves back to Scotland. They will eat a few lambs. That is nature's way. The farmers will complain. But then the mountains need the wolves. Without wolves there are too many sheep and deer on the hill and nothing other than grass and heather – no tree or shrub that pushes up above the heather – can grow.

'Thinking like a mountain' is what the American ecological prophet Aldo Leopold calls this – the mountain would like the wolves back because if it had some wolves the sheep would not get to eat all the trees before they grow tall and prevent the wind and rain from eroding the mountain. The mountains would also like the glaciers to remain and protect their rocks from being eroded by freeze and thaw. Last summer one Swiss mountain village was all but destroyed by a landslide from melting permafrost. And this is nothing to the effects of the loss of the glaciers of the Himalayas to the peoples of Tibet, Nepal, North India, and Pakistan who live off their meltwater.

---

33 Sources are myriad, e.g. Ahmad Khan, *Nigeria: The Political Economy of Oil* (Oxford: Oxford University Press, 1994).

Our civilisation stopped thinking like a mountain a long time ago. Jesus on the other hand often went to the mountain and the wilderness. Away from the people, in wild land not under human control, he could think and pray and be closer to his father in heaven.

We have mostly forgotten that we depend on the high places, the wild places – mangrove swamps, rainforests, glaciers, forests, mountain ranges. These are the great places of fecundity and fertility where life grows in all its diversity and where waters gather which nurture the plains. But we have cut down the trees, burned the mangroves, dried the swamps, and when the wood ran out we have mined the coal and drilled the oil that prehistoric mountain movements buried in the crust of the earth – and so when the rains come, the tsunamis rise up, and the storms strengthen, there is nothing to hold them back and they flood and wreak ruin in the cities.

The prophet Isaiah suggests that one day the earth will be released from the curse of empires like ours. When it is the 'forests will clap their hands and the hills will rejoice' (Isa. 55:12). At the same time as the cities are laid waste, the wilderness will flourish again and the rivers flow clean and full. And the poor will find justice in the wilderness while the palaces in the cities are stripped bare by jackals. But will this change, this reversal, only come through a global calamity?

We *can* change our way of living. Zac Goldsmith on Friday morning pointed out that in the 1880s all houses in the US and much of Europe were lit with whale oil. But the numbers of whales was declining, so savage had been the attacks on them from ports like Newhaven down the road. And so whale oil became too expensive. Everyone wondered what they would do. But within just 10 years all the whale oil lit homes were lit with a new fuel – fossil fuel. If we could make such a momentous change then, we could do it again. But it takes collective will.

The earth is judging us, not God. We do not need to be at war with the earth and yet we are. Some estimate the cost of the changeover to a renewable energy economy for the whole planet at upwards of 10 trillion dollars. But in the last 10 years the world has spent one trillion on arms *every year*. So in just ten years if we turned the arms industry into an energy industry we could save the planet without destroying our jobs and economies and societies.

How much judgment does it take?

But then the real problem is as a civilisation we don't believe in judgment any more, either divine or natural. Floods, droughts, and so on – these are not acts of God, or the revenge of Gaia, but random planetary perturbations

But this is not what the ancients believed. That is why I find it so significant that the editors of the Revised Common Lectionary tried to hide the judgment in our readings this morning. Even lambs know judgment.

I send you out as lambs among wolves.

32. Healing Hospitality

September 2003

So Naaman came with his horses and chariots, and halted at the entrance to Elisha's house. Elisha sent a message to him saying 'Go, wash in the Joran sevent times, and yor flesh shall be restored and you shall be clean.' But Naaman became angry and went away, saying, 'I thought that for me he would surely come out, and stand and call on the name of the Lord his God, and would wave his hand over the spot, and cure the leprosy!'

2 Kings 5:9–11

Lord, if you choose, you can make me clean.

Luke 5:12b

People are getting sick in British hospitals because hospitals are dirty. This is the news this week; it is tragic but predictable. Years ago the government followed private industry in extending the supply chain in the National Health Service and contracting out core services such as cleaning, catering, parking, and building maintenance to drive down costs. Cleaning was contracted out to private cleaning companies who pay staff on an hourly and temporary basis without full employment rights and with predictable results. British hospitals are now among the dirtiest in Europe.

The failure here is one of vision – of the nature of healing and therapy. The government imagines it is the technical interventions – the doctors and the drugs – that heal people. The cleanliness of the ward, the quality of the food, are epiphenomenal to that. The government even sets targets for the number of people a doctor will heal and to meet the targets the trust decides to clean floors less often. This is an elitist conception of healing – it indicates that experts heal while patients, and those who care for them and their surroundings, have only the most limited walk-on parts. It is also a classist conception – professionals are important, cleaners don't count. Pride in achievement, knowledge and technique has driven us down a road where hospitals are places where people often get ill even as others are healed.

Pride is also a central feature of our Old Testament reading today. The leper, Naaman, happens also to be a person of high position, one who is normally near the centre of the circle of insiders. His leprosy would normally make him automatically an outcast, but his high rank resists that expulsion. He is caught up in the games of mimetic rivalry, trying to hold on to and assert his rank. In fact, Naaman expects more respect from Elisha, thinking it beneath him to have to go wash seven times to be made clean. He becomes angry at Elisha's command. His servants, those already of lower station, convince him otherwise.

The leper in the story from Luke's Gospel is not angry or proud. Quite the opposite. He is not at all sure Jesus will be interested in him and so he asks the question 'Can you be bothered with me?' It is not the standard request for help, but reflects a genuine uncertainty about whether anyone could believe he deserved it. The man knows that Jesus is in control of his healing power, and can choose whether to heal or not, and we are told that his words moved Jesus.

When the healing is complete, Jesus sends the man straight off to register himself with the priest, so that he can be included again among his people. We are told that Jesus is 'stern' in his command that the man say nothing about the source of his healing. But the man cannot obey that command. It is simply beyond him. He is elated and uncontainable in his joy.

We do not know quite what he told people, but, whatever it was, it results in such fame for Jesus that he cannot go into the town anymore. Healing brings the leper back into his proper human community, but his witness to Jesus has the opposite effect. Jesus' power is already beginning to be costly, and to set him outside the community to whom he has come to proclaim the kingdom of God.

Note the significance of emotions in today's readings – the King is fearful, Naaman is angry, Jesus is 'moved with compassion' (Greek *splagchna*, which means in his guts). This progression of emotions is one that many of us will know, and especially the movement between fear and anger. Indeed many of us get stuck between these two emotions. Our fear and anger go within and become the seat of our own lack of wholeness.

The word for healing in the gospel today is the Greek word *katharizo*, from which we have the English word 'catharsis', though here it is translated cleanse. Jesus' acts of healing – and especially the one here described – are indeed cathartic. They address us those who receive them not only in the body but in the heart and mind. This holistic dimension to this story of healing challenges the modern mechanistic approach to medicine which treats the body but not the soul.

This holistic dimension also emerges from the social context of this story. For we are not talking only of individual healing but of social healing as well. Society fears the outcast – lepers, refugees, drug addicts. We make of them scapegoats for they help us to resolve our need to belong, which so often links to a desire to exclude others – a desire which goes right back to infancy when a mother's love was ours uniquely and we wrestled with the inclusion or exclusion of others from that inner circle of love.

This is why healing and hospitality have always been so central to the ministry of the Church from the earliest days in Jerusalem. 'Silver and gold have I none ...' The early Church is a religion of insiders – of those who loved each other deeply, so deeply that all traditional social divisions and exclusions were resolved, healed, reconciled – Greek–Jew, slave–free, man–woman.

This leads over time and in history to a movement of healing and hospitality which was beautifully symbolised in the medieval hostels for pilgrims to Canterbury, to Santiago de Compostella, to Rome and to Jerusalem. The hostels were the first hospitals. They were places of hospitality first and foremost, but over time they became specialised as places of healing.

In our own culture the specialisation has gone the other way round. If you spend time in a post-Thatcher NHS hospital you find the cleaners, the caterers, and increasingly even the nurses are contracted out, and work for an agency. The 'healing specialists' and the machinery of therapy are increasingly the only core functions left which are directly 'owned' or employed by the hospital.

This specialisation and splitting up of healing functions is reminiscent of a deeper problem with modern conventional medicine which regards each physical ailment as an ailment of only one bodily – mechanical – system. Connections between systems are mostly not considered and hence you go to a urologist or a cardiologist or a bowel surgeon or whatever. Similarly the design of the ward and the built environment of the hospital are not seen as intrinsically connected with the healing function. A new hospital building will often have a tin roof, and block and plasterboard walls, and be surrounded by treeless, privatised car parks. And the site is leased and maintained by private contractors with no investment in providing a healing environment. This division of functions can hardly make for a healing environment or a therapeutic community.

What has happened to our privatised hospitals is a manifestation of the deeper condition of our society. Outwardly, mechanically, we seem in the West to be in a better physical condition. But what about our inner lives? The number of people, including children, who are taking mind-altering drugs in our society is rising all the time. In California it is at epidemic proportions. But if California is the future, we are on the way there. What is going on?

Jesus looked in his healings to the whole person – he also looked at the illness as a manifestation of something in society. He knew that the skin disease of the leper was also an occasion of being socially outcast: it was this social disease which he healed, and symbolically challenged and overturned in his healing, as much as the physical ailment. In this story we find that sickness and *inhospitality*, healing and hospitality are closely connected. And this is why the word hospital has such a deeply Christian meaning even if a modern NHS hospital is the last place you might expect to get a good meal. And this is why we cannot as Christians contract out the healing of our bodies to a health care professional while neglecting the sources of unwholeness in our broken, money-oriented society.

And this is why as Christians we eat together every Sunday: at this table, in this Eucharistic feast is our healing, our hospitality because in this feast God and humanity sit down together, the ancient divide is healed, and friendship restored between God and persons. And so as you kneel to receive the bread and drink the wine of the kingdom today, before you do so offer up an element in your life at the altar for God's healing touch. It might be an unhealed relationship, it might be an unhealed memory, it might be a physical ailment. Bring your burden to the altar today and pray that God's Spirit will meet you in the bread and the wine, and that the healing sacrifice of Jesus will today make you and your loved ones whole, you and creation whole, you and this divided world whole.